Writing plots with drama, depth and heart:
NAIL YOUR NOVEL

Roz Morris

ISBN-13: 978-1-909905-98-6
ISBN-10: 1-909905-98-4

Okay, that's the warning stuff over. Now enjoy writing.

Electronic editions of this book are available from Amazon, Kobo,
Smashwords and the ibookstore
Cover image by LeoChen66 at iStockphoto.
Author photo by William Burton. Design by Roz Morris

www.nailyournovel.com

writing

plots

with

drama,
depth &
heart

Roz Morris

Also by Roz Morris

*Nail Your Novel: Why Writers Abandon Books
& How You Can Draft, Fix & Finish with Confidence*

*Writing Characters Who'll Keep Readers Captivated:
Nail Your Novel 2*

Fiction
My Memories of a Future Life
Lifeform Three

Contents

Introduction

In some ways it's false to split fiction-writing into departments of plot and character. The reader gets it as one organism – plot with character with style with setting with themes. But when coaching, writers' strengths and weaknesses tend to fall into these divisions so it's helpful to consider them separately. So if plot is your bete noir – or your keenest interest – this book is for you.

Drama, depth and heart

Why do we write fiction? Indeed, why do we read it? For a thrill, a chill, a world that is simpler, or more interesting, or cruel, or more loving or just. To laugh, to cry, to understand, to think, to forget, to remember. To – as Kurt Vonnegut said – meditate with the mind of another.

Of all the novelist's disciplines, the department of plot contains the most mechanical terminology and thinking. It's replete with theories of structure, forms, paradigms, plot points, conflict, classic journey shapes and tropes. Often these rules are made more complicated than they need to be, or appear to reduce storytelling to a soulless execution of formulae.

But they are attempts to understand how stories work, what makes them poignant, happy, uplifting, thrilling, enlarging, transforming. They are useful as a way to translate and scrutinise a complex reaction that takes place between the novel's text and the reader's mind. Knowing these ideas doesn't confine you to formulaic or simplistic stories, any more than knowing the laws of physics stops you being able to invent an aeroplane or a rocket that can travel to the moon.

In this book, I'm delving into what works, from two decades of dealing with raw writing, near misses and audacious triumphs – and helping writers create the effect they were striving for. It's not about rights and wrongs, it's about taking charge of your art – whether you write genre or literary fiction. I like this remark by the artist Mark Rothko: 'I'm not interested in colour or form. I'm interested in tragedy and doom.' Hold that thought.

An awareness book

This is a book to help you build your awareness as you write and edit. Is your plot intricate or impenetrable? Clever or contrived? New or nonsense? Often the distinctions are fine. I see a lot of manuscripts where the author has stabbed at an effect that hasn't worked – but would succeed with a tweak of character, or better foreshadowing, or a stronger subplot to direct the reader's receptiveness. You can have a dazzling prose voice and brilliant characters, but they won't hold us spellbound unless they do something that grabs – and keeps – our attention.

A book to help you revise

Much of the work on plot and story happens in revision. This is often a surprise to inexperienced writers. Many of my editing clients think revision is just about blitzing typos or finding a fine phrase. They're shocked when my report spends a half-page on their prose style, and twenty-nine on the physics of their story, how the characters could be tested more and whether they have kept the reader enmeshed.

One of my masterclass students shared a story that illustrates this. She described how she had come close to a publishing deal. The editors mentioned the book had problems and would need a thorough edit. Unfortunately, the imprint folded and she found herself on her own again. Worried that her book wasn't right, she embarked on more edits, and assumed the problems must lie with the style. So she worked to write the book in a more suitable way. Still, though, she was unhappy with it and didn't know why.

Editing veterans will be nodding sagely here, knowing that language is only one of many considerations when we revise. I've leaped into this trap myself. In the early days when I was querying agents with my first novel, I was told the book had a few rough areas. I made the only possible assumption – that I needed to improve the 'writing'. And so I fiddled, line by line, adding and pruning here and there. It was many years before I realised I

wasn't touching the real issues. I had no idea about the mecha-
nisms that work under the words, and that language is the skin on
top of the structure, pacing and character arcs. This is the guts of
the book. These are the devices that take charge of the reader's
emotions. The more we are aware of them, the better the novel
will work.

And so this is a revision book as much as a planning book or
a writing book. It will help you diagnose your story's strengths
and weaknesses. It will also help you if critique partners, beta
readers and editors remark that they didn't believe a story event,
or that the subplot was dull or the middle of the book was slow.

A book for the unconventional writer

Of course, you might want an unusual story. If so, bravo. The very
effect I'm warning against may be exactly what you want. and
conventional or not, all plots have certain qualities in common.
They offer an experience. There is a careful order to the events,
even if it isn't apparent to the reader. The reader's curiosity is
directed with clues and mysteries. If there is a cave in the woods,
or a man losing his dog, or a gun being loaded, or a couple having
a row, readers will hunt for the reason it is being shown. They will
seek connections with what has come before. They make a chain
in their mind. Good storytellers understand what breaks it and
what pulls a reader further in. Under the words, remember, is
where you do this – whatever your purposes.

Is it plot or is it story?

Plot and story are not the same, although I'll use them as syno-
nyms where the distinction doesn't matter. Strictly speaking, plot

is the events; story is what you make of them – which is part of the art. (And the fun.)

Who am I?

You'll have seen my novels in the bestseller charts, but you won't have seen my name because I was a ghostwriter, hired to write books as other people. I'm now coming out of the shadows with my own fiction. As well as writing, I have an extensive background in publishing and editing. I've run editorial departments. I've appraised manuscripts for a London literary consultancy and also as a freelance, and my clients include winners of prestigious national awards. I teach creative writing masterclasses for the *Guardian* newspaper in London. From my work with authors I wrote the other books in this series, *Nail Your Novel: Why Writers Abandon Books and How You Can Draft, Fix and Finish With Confidence,* and *Writing Characters Who'll Keep Readers Captivated.* Others are in the works.

Tragedy and doom (again)

Let's go back to Rothko. When I'm talking about structure or form, I'm striving for tragedy and doom. Or comedy, or romance, or complexity, or sadness, or wonder. I'm interested in the essence of what does this and how. Use this book to make your thrill, your suspense, your enlightenment, your exploration, your night of dark forces, your transformation, your drama, depth and heart.

Now let's explore.

1 Show not tell and why it rocks your plot

Show not tell is a fundamental dramatic principle. It is writing with the intention of giving the reader an experience.

Show not tell makes us feel as though we've been present as story events happen. It's persuasive when you need to teach us something about a character, an event or even an object. It's a great way to explain information to the reader in a way they will effortlessly remember.

It's also a memorable way to present back story. It can demonstrate how characters feel about each other, or how they hate the new town they've moved to (where something life-changing is going to happen, of course). In a nutshell, this principle makes a book vivid and alive.

Showing gets you more oomph out of your story events. It is the illusion that makes the reader forget they're looking at print. They're not reading, they're living alongside the characters, sharing their hopes, happinesses and disappointments. They're tasting the diesel fumes rising from a city street on a sweltering day as a character feels suffocated by the pressures in her life.

Showing requires more effort than planning and outlining, and a different mindset, which is one of the reasons writers need to be nudged about it. In our notes we might write 'the noise was frightening', but when we draft the scene we want the reader to taste the character's fear.

There are times, though, when telling is entirely appropriate. We have to be selective with what we present to the reader. It's not necessary to turn the emotion up for every scene. Not everything will be relevant to the emotional story. You might say 'John got up early' and what he felt about it doesn't matter.

And telling can have unexpected power. Occasionally, a dignified distance from an emotional scene strikes a better note than lingering close-ups. We'll discuss that later. But if you develop a habit of 'showing' as default, you won't go far wrong.

Here's how showing can improve your plotting and story.

'It was gorgeous' shows us nothing – character reactions summarised and therefore weakened

A character leaves her chaotic life to stay in a retreat in the Lake District. We're curious to know what her new life is like. The author writes:

> It was the most relaxing, enchanting place she'd ever
> known in her life.

That statement may be accurate, but what does it share with us? If this character's reaction is important, we don't want it swept aside in a few judgemental adjectives. Writers often say a place was 'relaxing', 'enchanting', 'uber-cool', 'quaint'. Or this:

> Her bedroom was garish and oriental, like something
> from a film.

But if you want us to see the bedroom, it's much more effective to give us details – perhaps a giant gold fan on the wall, a forest of red paper lanterns hanging from the ceiling, porcelain gods on the shelves, giant vases in the corners and dragon murals on a screen in the corner.

You could add 'garish and oriental' as a comment as well, if it fits with the narration or the narrator. Indeed it might underline your point nicely. But on its own it won't be as striking as the specifics. And if the bedroom was like a film set, who was the director? Cecil B DeMille's oriental bedroom would look startlingly different from one by the Coen brothers.

Quite often, you can solve the problem by asking yourself 'how'. Take these 'tell not show' lines:

> Adam was more worried than he had ever been.

How did Adam demonstrate this?

> Carlo was on her mind all the time.

In what way? Did every face in the crowd look like him?

> Peter didn't call; Jane wondered what it meant.

What did Jane wonder? How often did she wonder this? Take us through those thought processes and let us wonder alongside her.

Here's an example from real life. A friend took her four-month-old son to hospital for an operation. She said she coped with the major ordeals like having to starve him for twelve hours beforehand. But what really upset her – and surprised her – were the small details that she wasn't prepared for. Especially the moment where she had to pin down his struggling body and force the anaesthetist's mask onto his face. She could have said 'it was brutal'; instead she made me see the brutality. (All went well, BTW.)

Good writers strive for these truthful moments that will put us in the characters' shoes. In the words of Ernest Hemingway: 'It's your object to convey everything to the reader so that he remembers it not as a story he had read but something that happened to himself'.

Here's a fine example from fiction, which shows how words can put you in the experience. This is how Tim Winton writes a fatal car accident, in *Dirt Music*:

> There's dirt in his mouth. The sky gone completely.
>
> For a few moments Fox thinks he's gone to sleep, it's been a long, hot day and the travelling air is cool. But dead grass rasps against his cheek and a queer red light washes over the earth. Strange, but he thinks first of his mother, that he's there again on the ground beside her... He smells fuel, rolls over and is rent with the most abrupt pain like a hatchet high in the chest. God Almighty, he's out in the paddock...
>
> He gets to his knees and quickly understands that

> his collarbone is broken. Upright, arms crossed before him, he tries to take it in... He shambles across stony dirt to the drainage ditch where the ute's headlights burn into the ground... He blunders down to the up-turned one-tonner calling their names, all their names, revolted by the beetle-like underbelly of the vehicle, the evil turning of the rear wheel.

The telling version would be:

> Waking after the car had crashed was horrible; a dread-ful shock. It was painful when he got up. Walking hurt. He was aghast at what he saw...

I rest my case.

Instead of writing 'the day was traumatic', demonstrate how the day was traumatic..

What 'show not tell' is not

Show not tell is also misunderstood. It does not mean 'make a scene longer'. You can show in just a few lines or a short phrase. It also doesn't mean 'put this explanation into a character's mouth and have them say it as dialogue'. You can show without making characters speak.

Take this statement:

> Carlo was on her mind all the time.

Here's a way to convert this to showing while still being brief and staying with narration:

> She seemed to see Carlo a dozen times a day. A man

> with the same long-boned build was coming out of the
> Tube station, squinting at his phone. A man crossing at
> the lights had Carlo's wavy hair. At each of these
> moments she felt a twist of disappointment, as if fate
> had offered her another chance meeting with him and
> then pulled it away.

Show not tell is about the quality of the experience, the specifics.

Emotion, not action: Raymond Chandler

Here's a note about show not tell from Raymond Chandler.

> A long time ago when I was writing for pulps I put into
> a story a line like 'he got out of the car and walked
> across the sun-drenched sidewalk until the shadow of
> the awning over the entrance fell across his face like
> the touch of cool water.'
>
> They took it out when they published the story.
> Their readers didn't appreciate this sort of thing; just
> held up the action. And I set out to prove them wrong.
>
> My theory was they just thought they cared noth-
> ing about anything but the action; that really, although
> they didn't know it, they cared very little about the
> action. The things they really cared about, and that I
> cared about, were the creation of emotion through
> dialogue and description; the things they remembered,
> that haunted them, were not for example that a man got
> killed, but that in the moment of his death he was
> trying to pick a paper clip up off the polished surface

> of a desk, and it kept slipping away from him, so that
> there was a look of strain on his face and his mouth was
> half open in a kind of tormented grin, and the last thing
> in the world he thought about was death.
>
> He didn't even hear death knock on the door. That
> damn little paper clip kept slipping away from his
> fingers and he just couldn't push it to the edge of the
> desk and catch it as it fell.

The infuriating strain of trying to pick up a paper clip. The kind cruelty of pushing a mask onto your toddler's resisting face. The confusion after a car accident. The emotion is the experience.

When to tell

I said we'd look at telling again. Sometimes it's exactly what you need.

Most of the time we're trying to embed readers in the characters' experience. Distance (telling) diminishes that. But telling is useful where you don't want to give events too much emphasis.

You can write:

> John drove to Birmingham

if it's not important how that felt. You might even write

> John drove to Birmingham and was tired when he
> arrived

because the fatigue isn't one of the significant experiences of the story.

You might use telling to bridge a period that doesn't contain anything notable:

Ten minutes later, the knight was ready for battle.

But if a man was waiting on a lonely street corner to meet his lover because they were running away to Gretna Green, he might feel every moment keenly as he wonders if her courage might fail her. In that case, the empty minutes of agony might be worth emphasising.

You might also use telling to diminish the emotion, particularly to create irony, humour or whimsy. After all, comedy is often tragedy viewed at a distance.

Mr Crupper was out riding when a bee stung his mount. It bucked and he was dragged for two counties and as a result had a heart attack. And that is how young Fenella became, at the age of three, a duchess.

Of course, we must use distance carefully. I often see scenes where writers duck out of showing a key event, and it's usually because they were hoping to avoid writing it. There is a strong likelihood that if you pull the prose camera away from a pivotal scene, the reader will feel cheated – especially if there are questions lingering.

Telling can be a useful device. Enjoy it responsibly now, won't you?

If you want the reader to share the character's feelings, use showing. If that feeling isn't important, use telling.

For your toolbox

✎ Instead of writing 'the day was traumatic', demonstrate how the day was traumatic..

✎ 'Show not tell' does not mean 'make it longer'. It's about the quality of the experience, the specifics that make the reader feel they were present.

- If you want the reader to share the character's feelings, use showing. If that feeling isn't important, use telling.

2 Fundamentals of plot

It's tricky to set out ground rules about what a plot is. Storytelling is not a colour-by numbers exercise. It's an artform, full of exceptions that seem to make a nonsense of attempts to classify or define. With that in mind, there are certain fundamentals that help us understand how to build a satisfying plot.

Essentially, then, plot is what happens – a sequence of change. Let's look at the various shapes.

Straightforward hero journey

This is by far the most common type of story – a clear journey with a beginning, middle and end. A character begins by being confronted with a problem. The trouble escalates and the events are played out in chronological order, with many ordeals and rising tensions, both physical and emotional. There will be several 'acts' with twists, turns and a climax where the worst is confronted. Finally there is a resolution and a new order is created.

There is also the Joseph Campbell theory of story shapes, called the hero's journey or monomyth – a series of steps described in his book *The Hero With A Thousand Faces*. Briefly, Campbell describes how the vast majority of stories follow a similar pattern. A character leaves their ordinary life and enters a new world full of challenges and dangers. After many trials he returns, changed, and sometimes victorious. I'll discuss this in more detail later in the section on exercises to develop your plot (p176).

Although the hero's journey is a classic pattern, it doesn't have to be predictable. And dullness is not the fault of the structure or the convention, but of the way the story is done. In an absorbing story the template is invisible. The surprises are unexpected; the payoffs are interesting; the reader cares what happens.

Although simple, the straightforward hero journey is versatile and effective.

... and other kinds of plot

What other story forms could there be? Actually, the possibilities are endless. The basic journey described above is the simplest, but you could present your story in any number of ways. Here are a few.

The story of a life, from birth to death This form is organic, likely to be looser than the focused hero's journey.

The parallel plot You might have two parallel plots that will eventually merge. In Frederick Forsyth's *The Day of the Jackal*, one strand follows an assassin closing in on his target. The other concerns the police inspectors who are investigating rumours of a conspiracy, which leads them eventually to the assassin. Or you might have a parallel story connected by key characters. Andrew Miller's *Oxygen* concerns a translator who has returned to his childhood home to care for his dying mother and thus to confront the failures of his own life. He is translating a work by a revolutionary playwright – who, it turns out, has shameful regrets of his own. The reader is invited to notice the resonances between the plot strands, which give the novel its thematic thrust.

The ensemble plot You might not have one protagonist with one central problem; you might explore how one event or place affects the experiences of a large cast of characters. This is often used to explore cross-sections of society (Charles Dickens's novels have an ensemble element, as do family sagas) or a theme. Nevil Shute's *On The Beach* features an ensemble cast – the last people left alive as the world ends. Each has their individual way of facing their situation, which becomes a moving study of the human spirit. Max Brooks's *World War Z* is told by an ensemble of people whose accounts add up to a story.

The daisy chain This might be a series of separate stories that jump from one protagonist to the next, linked by an object that passes between them, or even a character. The journey usually gets its impact from contrast; perhaps by observing a cross-section of society (like the ensemble plot) or chronicling a historical period if the linking item is longlived. *Dracula* and *The Woman in White* have this form, handing the baton of the story on.

Reverse chronology This is an unusual one, but a fine example of creative plotting. In *Time's Arrow*, Martin Amis tells the story of a concentration camp guard, starting from his death. As the story progresses he gets younger, passing from retirement, to practising medicine, to fleeing to America, to his time in Auschwitz. The reverse presentation creates an unsettling logic, as the character simply accepts that when he has been to see a doctor he must wait in a room for an hour afterwards. Relationships begin with arguments that fade into blissful romances. Doctors cause injuries, which are healed by blows. And in the Auschwitz years, people are created from the clouds, nourished, and sent into the world. This startling treatment of events creates many effects, among them a sense of persistent misinterpretation.

The challenging plot To generalise vastly, this is the antithesis of the conventions that appear in the straightforward story sequence. So usually, the writer places clues so that they are memorable, although disguised. Most of the events and characters are relevant, even though we won't realise it at the time. Timelines are clear. We know when scenes are set and where they're taking place. We know what is real and what's a dream sequence, or a fantasy or a flashback. But some writers aim to challenge more – and readers of these stories enjoy the effort and immersion needed to grasp the big picture. Their novel may be full of details that seem digressive or superfluous; character perspectives that seem irrelevant or unclear; plotlines or timelines that shift around and make you wonder where you are, or if you're reading a dream or a fantasy. This kind of novel is often called plotless because it seems hard to access, but in fact there's a lot going on; there are plenty of changes and challenges to the characters. An example is Mark Z Danielewski's *House of Leaves*, which contains copious footnotes (including footnotes to the footnotes), references to fictional films and books, unconventional page layouts with some pages crowded and others a sparse line or two, and multiple narrators who interact in elaborate and disorientating ways.

The minutiae stream of consciousness The stream-of-consciousness narrative will be full of mundanities and everyday happenings that in more conventional plots might seem digressive or too ordinary. The power of this kind of plot is the immersion, the experience of losing yourself in the world of another.

If you want to explore interesting structures in your novel, there's an exercise in the fun and games department (p186).

It's interesting to note that although these story forms may seem loose and unordered, they still deliver a sequence of change and a journey. Many of them also conform to the classic three-act structure. We'll revisit structure in a later chapter.

Four Cs for a good plot: curiosity, crescendo, coherence and change

With such a variety of story types, can we identify any common features that all plots have?

Yes we can. (Although if we're deliberately constructing the challenging plot, all bets are off.)

Curiosity They make the reader curious. Perhaps the characters are venturing to challenging places. Or something is unstable or wrong in their lives. We often hear the term 'promise of the premise', or the promise to the reader. This is it: early in the story, there is something that hooks the reader. And however simple the problem – or quest – seems at the start, it proves tricky to solve and there are many twists and turns. This is why it is a long story, not a short one.

Crescendo Stories have crescendoes. The situation gets bad, and then much worse. There are times where the trouble reaches a turning point and spins it off somewhere new. There may also be triumphs.

Coherence Readers adore stories that have coherent themes and ideas, even if the form is looser than the traditional sequence of beginning-middle-end. If the writer can make the reader believe everything in the story has a worthwhile place and operates together, the novel will look elegant and confident (perhaps that's another C).

Change A satisfying plot also gives a feeling of change, a sense of a journey. The action might take us through many locations. The characters might complete a series of challenges or tasks. There will also be changes in their understanding – and in the reader's. As the story progresses, there is a sense of finality. There's no undoing what's been done. Irrevocable things have happened – for instance, a divorce, or a death, or a character has travelled to the Moon. There may be a 'no return' factor in the characters' personalities. Perhaps the ordeal would stop if they backed down or gave up, but they can't because they are stubborn, or honourable, or trapped, or a promise has been made.

The four Cs for a good plot are curiosity, crescendo, coherence and change.

Four questions to identify your genre – and how you should handle your plot

Spoiler alert: *The Fear Index*, Robert Harris

Most story situations could be handled hundreds of ways. A quest, at its heart, is not that different from a mystery. Any plot might start with a protagonist transported to a new place, or returning home and finding it changed. Any plot might involve danger, love or death. There are infinite ways to shuffle and emphasise.

Your genre governs how you treat your story ideas. And this comes from where your curiosity lies.

Do you like to dissect characters, revelling in observations of their interior states? Are those more interesting to you than the external events? Do you enjoy the ambiguities and qualities of the human condition more than answers and solutions? Then you have a literary bent. Of course, literary is a quality, an approach, and may be blended with other kinds of story. Ray Bradbury's *Fahrenheit 451* is at once literary fiction and science fiction.

Do you get your kicks from what happens, rather than from insights into humanity? Then you're more suited to the fast-paced, tightly plotted genres, such as thrillers, action-adventure, murder mystery or crime. However, that doesn't mean you can't draw characters who are complex and lifelike. But the reader will demand action as well.

Do you like stories that arise from the challenges and charms of particular settings? For instance, historical periods, the Wild West, science fiction or fantasy worlds? There's another clue to your genre.

Do you like a particular kind of ending? In certain genres, readers aren't satisfied unless the story has brought the characters to a particular outcome. Romance must pair the correct lovers or split them up for ever. A thriller will usually see the world saved or restored to equilibrium, although the truce might be unstable (like Robert Harris's *The Fear Index*). Cosy murder must bring the killer to justice. Indeed, murder is an interesting question to consider. In a different genre, the killer might not be found, or they might go free. Or the murder might be peripheral, while the story explores many other things. Perhaps you like an ending to surprise and challenge you, to follow where the author leads. If so, you might not be suited to a genre that needs a particular outcome.

These conventions don't mean your story is formulaic or predictable. Part of your skill – and your signature – is how you satisfy the reader while doing your own thing. You might bend your genre's traditions – put dinosaurs in a thriller (Michael Crichton's *Jurassic Park*), make comedy out of its tropes (*Bored of the Rings*; Terry Pratchett and Discworld), add a fantasy or paranormal slant (*Twilight*). Or reimagine a fairytale as science fiction (*Cinder*, by Marissa Meyer). Or put zombies or Jane Austen with almost anything. (Or together, if you really must.)

Discover the genre you should write by examining your own tastes.

Finding coherence

As we said earlier, readers love the elegant, tight story. Here are tips for staying streamlined.

Explore repercussions, reactions and consequences Some manuscripts contain juicy developments that go unexplored. Instead of adding a new idea, check whether an existing one could be pushed further.

See if you can reintroduce something you've already used If you bring back a detail the reader thinks you've finished with, you cause much delight. This might be a character, a location, or maybe a skill your main character used in the early part of the story.

As with most storytelling principles, this is a reflection of what works in real life, so here's a non-bookish example. At a surreal supper event in London, the guests ate hors d'oeuvres served in paper cake cases tethered to helium balloons, which then floated up to the ceiling, causing gasps of delight. Between courses, the guests played a consequences storytelling game. After pudding (a suitably surrealist baked Alaska) they took turns to read out the resulting lunacy – while breathing in the helium from the balloons.

Isn't there something amazingly right about bringing them back? We'd forgotten them in all the other charming foolery, but they were bobbing on the ceiling all along, present but not noticed.

This is called reincorporation. It is primevally satisfying. When you're tempted to invent more events or characters, look for something you could bring back in. Did you send your character to a meeting, perhaps because you needed a reason why he wasn't at home? Use it when he needs a hobby, or a place to overhear a vital piece of gossip. Did you use an anecdote about an unwise hobby for character building? Make it the means by which he saves the day – or kills the neighbour's dog. Push something to the audience's peripheral vision – or make it look as though you have finished with it. Then whisk it out again with a flourish.

But don't do this more than once. What's smart first time can become like the tough villain who tediously won't die. However, because repetition is very noticable, you can repeat the reincorporation if you have a clear artistic aim, such as creating the sense of a curse, or reinforcing an idea of fate or bad luck.

Create a sense of progress We've talked a lot about the value of change in a story and how readers love a sense of transformation. Again, this comes from developing events, mysteries or intrigues, rather than adding new ones.

Every event you invent, ask if you can make more use of it. Then you are on the way to an elegantly crafted story with focus and coherence.

For your toolbox

✎ The straightforward hero journey is simple, but it is versatile and effective.

✎ Although less simple story forms may seem looser than the straightforward plot, they still deliver a sequence of change and a journey. Many of them also conform to the classic three-act structure.

✎ The four Cs for a good plot are curiosity, crescendo, coherence and change.

✎ Discover the genre you should write by examining your own tastes.

✎ Every event you invent, ask if you can make more use of it. Then you are on the way to an elegantly crafted story with focus and coherence.

3 Where plots come from

In my characters book I have a section called 'why plots happen –
motivation, need and conflict'. Here's the companion discussion.
But in a nutshell: plots come from unstable situations.

Plot from setting and the novel's world

Spoiler alert: *The Ghost*, Robert Harris

One of the most significant sources of plot is the novel's setting,
and the tasks characters do from day to day. Detectives always
have murders to solve, adulterers to spy on, missing people to find,
thieves to thwart or stolen treasures to recover. Doctors have
moral dilemmas, medical conundrums that highlight the human

condition or require them to be brave and brutal. Airline pilots, ambulance drivers and even car mechanics have the responsibility of people's lives.

In fantasy, science fiction, historical fiction and Wild West fiction, stories are generated from situations that are characteristic of the time and place. In suburbia, plots come from the fundamentals of everyday life, from the 'normal' going wrong – or from the characters' attempts to fit in.

How old are your characters? In contemporary fiction, child characters might have troublesome parents, school situations or friends. Teenage characters will have all this and extra freight from newly turbulent relationships, body image and their views about their future.

Each stage of life provides challenges that can feed stories – leaving college, becoming a parent, watching the children move away, changing career and getting old. A character of any age might face the death of a partner or be cut adrift from home and safety.

A geographical neighbourhood might contain a cross-section of humanity that can mix to make a story. Ruth Rendell's *The Keys to The Street* is set in London's Regent's Park and covers the intertwined fates of a down-and-out, the former butler to a rich tycoon and a fragile divorcee who is preyed on by a con man.

Any special world might take a character into danger. Robert Harris's thriller *The Ghost* is about an author who is ghostwriting the memoirs of a British prime minister. The narrator is filling the shoes of a previous ghostwriter, who was found dead in mysterious circumstances. Soon he suspects his predecessor was murdered, and discovers clues that the ex-PM was involved in war crimes. The conflict escalates and the ghostwriter must juggle several requirements: his obligation to finish the job; his desire to collect the hefty fee; the moral need to uncover and tell the truth; the emotional need to protect some of the people caught up in the PM's story; and the need to get out alive at the end.

Indeed, some settings make a promise in themselves. If you write about the circus, readers will expect danger, unusual people, life on the road, physical courage, high wires and fire-eating. I see quite a few manuscripts where the writer has failed to deliver on those basics.

Don't miss the plot potential in your story's setting and world.

Plot from character flaws and relationships: *Revolutionary Road*

Spoiler alert

So much for external pressures and challenges. But interesting pressures also come from within. Characters in the most ordinary, safe circumstances can generate compelling plots purely by being their flawed, imperfect selves.

Richard Yates's novel *Revolutionary Road* centres on Frank and April, a bright young couple who are bored by the banalities of suburban life and long to be extraordinary. Yates packs the story with twists and turns that are surprising, inevitable and riveting – and arise from a deep understanding of the characters' inner issues.

Early in the novel, Frank takes a secretary out on his birthday and seduces her. We're expecting this will be the start of a descent into secret philandering because his marriage has gone sour. And that would be interesting, but...

A twist When he goes home, April has had enough too. She's realised Frank is crushed and trapped and suggests they sell up and move to Paris, where they can become the people they dreamed of being. (And she's braver and more clever than him; a nice foreshadowing of how eventually, Frank isn't clever or brave enough, and certainly not as brave and clever as he wants to be.)

They are rejuvenated by the plan. Neighbours and colleagues are jealous. Frank and April are like honeymooners again. Frank is having grandiose fantasies about his last day at work, breezing through assignments with new-found bravado because he doesn't care if he gets in trouble. He boasts to colleagues. April has come alive for the first time in years. We're expecting that something must go wrong.

A twist The children start to get anxious about leaving. Frank seizes on it. We suddenly see he was afraid of going too. The person who will torpedo this plan is Frank himself.

Frank is praised by his boss for a piece of work he tossed off with contempt. We wonder – will he use this to tell April maybe it's not so bad in the US after all? And that would certainly cause trouble but then…

A twist April falls pregnant. That second-honeymoon humping has paid unexpected dividends. Suddenly Frank has a lifeline. But even better, April is bitterly upset and wants to abort it. She has two weeks to make up her mind. (A deadline in a story is always good for adding pressure.) Frank has to delay her with wooing and sweet-talking until she is twelve weeks gone. Otherwise he will have to go to France.

A little later, the danger is over and April has kept the child. Frank is in the clear. He can stay in his job, where he is flying higher than ever. By this point, the knots Frank has tied himself in start to tighten. He has a meeting with the big boss at headquarters.

It's a hot day and he goes to the exec's office imagining a plush suite with aircon and fine furniture. Actually, it's a shabby box room, just like the crowded cubicle hell he works in. Instead of feeling liberated, Frank feels trapped in the same old place. Worse, now that April can no longer abort, Frank realises he doesn't want another child.

The situations are so ironic and skewed:

- Frank spends his life wanting things, and as soon as he gets them they are a trap.
- He sleepwalks through his days, imagining he is built for finer things but never has the backbone to follow his dream. He also hates himself for it.
- He screws his secretary and when he comes home his wife throws him a lifeline to save his soul.
- He has the chance to find himself – and then he has to get out of it.
- He has to keep his wife sweet to persuade her not to abort his child.

The novel is full of complications, big changes and mess – and it all comes from a deep understanding of the characters' psychology, what they think they want and what they actually want underneath that. Especially Frank; for him this is the most important confrontation of his life.

And the end? I won't reveal it because you need to enjoy it on its own terms. Does Frank get rid of his central conflict? On a superficial level he does. On a deeper level he's buried it more completely than ever. This is a fine example of a story where resolution is not always a case of besting your inner demons.

Look for plot potential in your characters' psychological fault lines, their relationships and their illusions about themselves.

Plot from theme

Novels are given weight by their themes, universal questions that will keep the reader puzzling about rights, wrongs and grey areas. Themes give a novel a wider resonance and relevance than just the story events. If you identify the main themes in your novel, you can use them to generate more events and subplots, and they'll seem to fit naturally, like harmonising notes in a musical chord. So if you need to flesh out a story about envy, add some events and subplots that illustrate another form of envy and the reader will feel a sense of rightness and depth.

William Golding's *Lord of the Flies* generates some of its plot from the story situation –a group of schoolboys shipwrecked on a deserted island, struggling to survive. Other story events are thrown up by the personalities of the characters – the factions that form, the varying ways the boys handle the threat of real, life-or-death danger. And some events confront the fundamental thematic questions – particularly about 'civilising' influences such as safety, comfort and adult supervision.

Find your novel's themes and use them to enrich the storyline.

What's your story really *About*?
Story metaphor, symbols and themes

Every now and then, a writer will be asked: 'what's your novel about'?

There are two ways to answer. The situation: 'it's about a school reunion'. And the themes and concerns (perhaps pronouncing the word with special emphasis): 'it's *About* memory, regret and friendships'.

How do we tap into this second dimension, the About with a

capital A? How do we make sure the reader notices we're tackling a universal struggle?

We have to use a light touch. I see manuscripts where the writer is desperate to point out their clever parallels. There are many scenes where the characters do A Meaningful Thing such as fishing, where nothing happens except aimless bait-dangling, and we know by the strangely ponderous gap in the action that the writer is saying 'Do you get it? Do you understand my metaphor for life?'

Although story metaphor, symbols and themes are not the same things, they do have a common quality – they work best when they are covert, not lit in neon.

When a theme, symbol or metaphor is handled well, the reader uncovers it for themselves. They are not constantly reminded what fishing represents, however they are aware it is an ordering force. Therefore the story must work on its own terms first. A metaphor – or theme – that is too obviously operating the story is unnatural. It's the author turning the characters into puppets to ram home the message.

So if you want your characters to go fishing as a symbolic act, make it real in the story world. Give them a reason to do it – perhaps it is their restorative escape. Knit it into the relationships, so that fishing is a key way that characters bond – or fall out.

Novels that explore ideas do it best through people's behaviour. If you want your book to reflect Jungian theory, make the material into compelling stories about individuals and let the novel's world operate according to Jungian principles. Examine what Jung makes you feel about the order of the universe – and create a story that shares those impressions with the reader. If you have a fascinating theme, consider what kind of people get into trouble because of it, and what they might do. Search for gripping dilemmas. (This is also how you say something new and discernibly your own.)

Although themes add meaning and depth, we don't want them to be a leaden weight. If you examined *Nineteen Eighty-Four* it would be hard to spot whether the love story arose because it's a compelling way to tackle the themes of freedom and the individual, or whether Orwell had an idea for a love story in an oppressed world and wanted to explore the questions it raised. (However, Orwell does bring the entire story to a halt with a long tract of thesis in Emmanuel Goldstein's forbidden book. For many readers, it's too heavy handed.)

AS Byatt, interviewed about her novel *Possession*, explained that she started with the idea that a dead writer could possess the lives of the people who study him. The title came quickly, and so did other ideas about possession – especially in relationships. Byatt said she was originally planning to write an experimental novel that would juxtapose glimpses of poets and lovers through a series of theoretical texts and biographical material – a presentation of her theme for readers to study. But then she read Umberto Eco's *The Name of the Rose*, and noticed how readers were enjoying the medieval theology alongside the parodic detective story. She says: 'The secret, I saw, was that if you tell a strong story, you can include anything else you need to include. So I started inventing a detective story.'

She invented a story. I feel that deserves italics. Once you've identified the theme or metaphor, you need to get over how clever you were and concentrate on the story. Theme is not, by itself, a story. Metaphors and themes are there to enhance a good story. And they'll usually sink a weak one.

Remember 'show not tell', the novelist's essential. Essays tell us facts or ideas; a novel turns them into life. The playwright Harold Pinter liked to write from the main dramatic events backwards. Instead of starting with themes, he allowed them to emerge as the story took shape. Orwell's *Animal Farm* works because it is presented as weirdly plausible. We immerse in the characters and events – and breathe in the parallels that occur to us as we read.

There always are these two levels to a good story, a deeper core than just the plot and characters. Themes are like a subconscious force, guiding the writer's choice of characters and plots, giving it an intriguing and recurring shape. But they're not overtly in control of what's going on.

Themes are almost a pattern seen by outsiders, a consideration for critics and readers, not for the surface. The story can become stilted and inhibited if the author thinks in terms of abstract forces and patterns, instead of people.

So let's get back to about and About. H Rider Haggard's *She* is a simple adventure story, but it also explores questions of whether you'd want to live for ever. *King Lear* is about a pair of skewed families. It's About man at the mercy of a chaotic universe. *Othello* is about a proud man who decides to take revenge on another proud man, and it's About jealousy and a descent into evil. *Revolutionary Road* is about several people who wish they had made more of their lives and it's About the failure of the American dream.

We have two levels here. The lower-case 'about' is characters and stories. Capitalised 'About' shimmers out of that. Your theme may be immediately apparent to you, or it may not be clear until you've driven the story around the block several times. Once you are aware of it you can let it trickle though in imagery, scene-setting and texture (as Shakespeare does, for example, with Lear's storm). But don't let it become the plot or a substitute for a plot.

Write what your story is 'about' and let 'About' take care of itself.

Other ways to overstate themes

Here are two other ways that writers get heavy-handed with theme.

Dialogue The characters have a tendency to discuss and highlight the theme in an unnatural way. In a scene where we'd expect them to gossip about another character, or the movie they just saw or the trip they're about to make, they have an earnest discussion about thematic issues. If the book's underlying concern is the oppression of minorities, the characters discuss it on the faintest excuse.

Wallpaper The world of the novel becomes a billboard for the themes. Every available medium is used to advertise the author's angles. If the characters watch TV, read a book or newspaper, comment on Twitter – the theme is the only question the world is thinking about. Unless there's a reason for this – for instance, the world is enthralled by the Moon landings – it becomes clear that the author is mounting a campaign for attention.

Of course, there are natural ways for characters to talk about a thematic topic. A great way is to use it for subtext, make it code for something else. For instance, strangers at a party might chat about genetic engineering to get the conversation going. But even so, some of the characters will be less interested in genetic engineering than others, and we'll detect they have more pressing agendas, such as: showing off; gauging whether a rival is more successful than them; angling to be introduced to an influential person or wondering whether they can slope off home. If you use a strangers' conversation as an opportunity to explore your theme, look also for these elements of ulterior motive and undercurrent. Stay in the story – the real heart of the scene should be their own desires and personalities.

Beware of overstating your theme in dialogue and the story's wallpaper.

Statement of theme: the nucleus moment

Spoiler alert: *Any Human Heart,* William Boyd

Having said all the above, there are times when the reader relishes a moment when a line seems breathtakingly resonant, seeming to fix the nucleus of the book in one sentence: the statement of theme.

Graham Swift's *Waterland* is a complex narrative that loops through several timelines – the narrator's teenage years; his troubled life now he's in his fifties; the history of his mother's family and the lives of the people who shaped the Fens. The narrator is a history teacher who is haunted by his past while he battles to convince his headmaster – and pupils – that history still has relevance. There's much more besides, but one line acts as a drawstring that pulls these ideas tightly around him:

> Often the future we dream of is built upon the dreams
> of a long imagined past.

Here's another example, from the film *Groundhog Day*, where a TV weatherman relives the same twenty-four hours over and again. He utters this line, which is comic, but also central to how his life feels:

> What if there is no tomorrow? There wasn't one today.

Sometimes the statement of theme explains the title, or even contains it. William Boyd does this, near the end of *Any Human Heart*. The narrator, who has become quite elderly, is at the doctor's surgery after a suspected coronary. The doctor is telling him, gently, that such things are an inevitable consequence of ageing:

> Look at your face in the mirror, and consider how it has
> changed. Think of your old heart as like your old face...
> Imagine that everything that has happened to your face
> over the years has happened to your heart.

Indeed it has, and that line has a special, powerful meaning for us as we have taken that journey with him.

As with all mutterings from the theme level of the story, such a moment should look natural, as though the character has had a rare flash of insight. The nucleus moment is like someone saying 'story of my life'. It might deepen the puzzle or give the character an ease, an answer.

Wherever you put your nucleus moment, the reader must have enough background to appreciate its full meaning. It is a moment of personal enlightenment for the character and also the reader.

It's often good if deployed at a point where the reader is expecting an emotional peak or turning point, a fundamental change in the character's priorities or understanding. There are a number of sweet spots for these changes and we'll discuss them later in the section on structure (p117).

A nucleus moment requires a long, intimate, honest relationship with the reader. It must seem special, a remark for insiders only. If you put it too early, the reader might miss it or think it self-conscious or artificial.

Indeed a great nucleus moment can create a turning point of such power and coherence that it is like a fine plot twist – which is why it is worth discussing in a book about plot. William Boyd deploys his nucleus moment when he's just pages from the end – the leave-taking phase that lets the reader dwell on the novel's implications. *Any Human Heart* is otherwise a loosely structured book as it is intended to resemble a set of diaries (although I'll discuss its structure in more detail later). To create a conventional climax would be artificial, but by including this sequence with its haunting line Boyd is able to create a single point of great impact. If you read the novel you will never forget it.

If your novel has several themes or a loose structure, could you make use of a nucleus moment?

Challenge your themes, issues and messages

If your story has a theme or a message, it's tempting to make the case for it strongly and incessantly. But if you do that, you risk browbeating the reader. Instead of accepting your thesis, they may feel it's being forced on them – even if the 'message' seems clear cut or indisputably right. However, if you introduce a note of dissent, the reader will feel they are free to make up their own mind.

Novels are emotional. You want to get the reader rooting for your cause, not just agreeing with you. So if you're exploring the waste and horror of the World War I trenches, you might do this by showing a much-loved character being killed. Certainly that's powerful, but it's a tad obvious. But what about a scene where, for example, the captain reports back to a general at HQ and tells him the men are ill equipped. The general replies by complaining that his fine wines are all shaken up and his cigars are damp. Finally he suggests that the men at the front should have more backbone. By introducing a contrary point of view, you can make the reader's blood boil.

Be daring. If you want to explore rape, include a scene where somebody suggests the victim was asking for it. Or have a rapist escape unpunished. The reader will be so outraged that they will commit to your cause and your characters. You'll also add conflict by giving the heroes a bigger problem to tackle – which is no bad thing. More about conflict later (p52).

If your novel has an issue or message, challenge it to make it stronger.

Bursting at the themes: writer tries to cram in all possible ramifications

Sometimes writers seem desperate to include every ramification of their theme. The characters endure an unbelievable set of misfortunes just to cover every possibility – but the book doesn't work as a whole and the threads can't be brought to a satisfying conclusion.

Part of writing is deciding what to leave out. There will always be ideas you don't have room for and thematic dimensions you can't explore.

Here's where subplots can be useful. You can give your spare events to another cohort of characters; put them through a complementary set of trials that will help unify your novel. But sometimes even this isn't possible, so we have to let ideas go. Accept that the reader will understand that under the water the iceberg is a lot bigger. That's how universality works anyway. We can see to the edge of the galaxy, but we know there's a whole lot more out there.

Don't bend the story to shoehorn something in, no matter how thematically resonant it is. Remember our four Cs – a coherent story has more power than a sprawling, messy one.

Are you trying to squeeze too many thematic variations into your story?

Only here for the Lear: a pitfall when creating a plot from significant literary parallels

Some novels get their plot and structure from echoing a more famous work. The novel is enriched by the parallels, similarities and departures from the original.

But some manuscripts seem inhibited by this instead of inspired. The writers seem reluctant to invent new plot events and characters so the narrative seems flat and uninvolving – maybe even preachy. They might be self-conscious about the origins, with characters who are unrealistically prone to comparing themselves to Hamlet, Tess Durbeyfield or Catherine Earnshaw.

Of course, there are times when this might have a good story reason. Geraldine McCaughrean's *White Darkness* features a narrator who frequently mentions the explorer Titus Oates, and indeed embarks on an expedition to Antarctica. In *White Darkness*, this is a believable character trait because she has created Oates as a fantasy idol to compensate for other problems. Without this story reason it would look artificial. No matter how august the source text is, you should still create a fiction of your own (unless you're aiming to be experimental).

Use the comparisons when they will fit naturally, but don't be afraid to depart.

Jane Smiley's *A Thousand Acres* is derived from *King Lear* but there are as many differences as similarities. The initial situation is the same – a domineering father decides to hand over his kingdom to his daughters. In Smiley's update the kingdom is a Midwest farm rather than a country. The names have clear echoes. Lear becomes Larry Cook. Daughters Goneril, Regan and Cordelia become Ginny, Rose and Caroline. Caroline is disowned early in the story, as Cordelia is. Ginny and Rose end up as rivals, as Goneril and Regan do. Other key cast members are reimagined from Shakespeare's play. Lear/Larry has a wise friend whose loyalty will be pushed to the limit.

Smiley explores similar ideas to Shakespeare's original – loyalty, betrayal, family favour, familial cruelty and infidelity, but she updates it with current issues of marital happiness, career and fertility. In Shakespeare's story, Lear's friend (the Earl of Gloucester) has two sons – Edgar, his heir, and Edmund, who is an outcast because he is illegitimate. Legitimacy isn't such a concern in Smiley's narrative, so she creates a dutiful son who stays at home to take over his father's farm and an adventuring son who causes upset. This allows her to examine duty and loyalty in a modern context.

Another famous reworked classic is *Bridget Jones's Diary* by Helen Fielding, which follows the plot and characters of *Pride and Prejudice*. Parallels with the original abound. Part of the fun is to spot the character personalities, names, locations and plot events that unabashedly echo Jane Austen's original. But we are intended to engage with them as their own people too, and become caught in their own new story. Bridget is as real as Lizzie Bennet.

Use an origin work to provide contrast, texture, echoes, questions, themes and symbols, but make sure the novel can also function without this backdrop. Don't make the parallels more important than your characters and what is happening to them.

For your toolbox

- Don't miss the plot potential in your story's setting and world.
- Look for plot potential in your characters' psychological fault lines, their relationships and their illusions about themselves.
- Find your novel's themes and use them to enrich the storyline.
- Write what your story is 'about' and let 'About' take care of itself.
- Beware of overstating your theme in dialogue and the story's wallpaper.
- If your novel has several themes or a loose structure, could you make use of a nucleus moment?
- If your novel has an issue or message, challenge it to make it stronger.
- Are you trying to squeeze too many thematic variations into your story?
- Use an origin work to provide contrast, texture, echoes, questions, themes and symbols, but make sure the novel can also function independently. Don't make the parallels more important than your characters and what is happening to them.

4 Conflict, stakes and plot: are you looking for trouble?

Remember we defined a plot as a sequence of change? Good plots also have a sense of strife and instability. This comes from conflict.

Many writers – including some of great experience and reputation – find plotting difficult because they don't look keenly enough for conflict. Or they fail to spot how much conflict they can squeeze out of their plot situation. Or they create one gripping central conflict, but miss opportunities to develop it elsewhere, leaving the rest of the novel rather superficial – or indeed short. When I'm writing an editor's report, one of the most significant sections will be headed 'you could generate more conflict here'.

What do we mean by conflict? It's a situation of disruption that causes a struggle. Simple as that. And where might conflict come from?

- *People* Opponents and antagonists, friends, the characters' own dilemmas
- *The plot situation* Any troublesome event – a war, an apocalypse, a hostile or dangerous environment, a death in the family, a divorce, a job loss, a murder, a mystery, a lottery win.

In *Nineteen Eighty-Four* a man starts to write a diary because he needs an escape from his bleak life. Is that a big deal? Well it is for him, because writing a diary breaks most of his society's rules, so he must keep it secret. The secret writing of it awakens an awareness that makes it impossible for him to accept his society's rules – and yet he cannot stop.

Here's a lighter-hearted example: in Sophie Kinsella's *Confessions of a Shopaholic,* a young woman realises she is getting into debt. This makes her miserable, so she cheers herself up with an expensive designer handbag. She is in a circle of conflict that will cause considerable trouble.

In *The Pilot's Wife* by Anita Shreve, a woman is told by police that her husband has been killed in a plane crash. From this one bad event, the author conjures up a chain of conflicts that enrich the plot and complicate an already tragic situation. Not only does the protagonist have to cope with her husband's death, she must help the police investigate him because there are suspicious circumstances. Her distress increases as unpleasant secrets are discovered. Her teenage daughter blames her. The newspapers hound her because her husband was flying a passenger plane and they sniff a scandal. From this one awful situation, the author has teased out every possible thread of conflict to keep the storyline bubbling.

Good story writers have a nose for conflict. And it often takes several drafts or outlines to find and exploit it. We need to heap trouble on trouble, keep pushing the characters into their worst nightmares and beyond.

We can also find conflict inside the characters, especially in literary or slice-of-life novels – so their personalities, hopes, dreams, fears, mental issues and resentments might make a simple problem into a major issue (as we saw in *Revolutionary Road*, where events that might be joyous for some people are major obstacles for the viewpoint character Frank).

Broadly speaking, there are four classic general conflict areas. These are the hero versus:

- themselves
- society
- the environment or nature
- other characters, who are competing for the same thing as the hero, or who might spoil the hero's happiness, or stop him achieving his goal.

This brings me to the close cousin of conflict: stakes. Whatever problems you generate for the characters, they won't grab the reader's curiosity unless they seem to matter. So let's discuss that.

Making the conflict matter: stakes

If conflict is a struggle, a situation of strain, we must make the reader understand why the characters are compelled to endure it. After all, why live under such stress?

Faulty plots often fail to answer this. So the character has a secret past that they must keep hidden, but we don't appreciate why this is so important.

Just like plot goals, good story conflicts have two parts. First is the unstable situation itself – a tightrope, if you will. Second is the chasm that beckons if the character falls.

So – a man is in love with the fiancée of his son (Josephine Hart, *Damage*). What are the stakes? His stable family will be destroyed if the secret is discovered. However, he can't give his lover up; he is obsessed. And so the conflict situation continues, on that horrible tightrope.

Soon after Winston Smith starts his diary in *Nineteen Eighty-Four*, we see how merciless the society is to people who don't toe the line. Orwell gives us plenty of examples. One of Winston's neighbours is in fear that her own children will misinterpret something she has done and report her to the authorities – a common scenario in this off-kilter world. We see the risk Winston runs by his subversive acts – first the diary, then later when he takes a lover. But we also know that he can't stop.

Conflict and stakes will be determined largely by the novel's genre. In a thriller, the external conflict may be caused by an antagonist. The stakes will be human lives, which the hero must save without getting killed himself. In a comedy the stakes are usually the hero's dignity and happiness. In teen fiction, the stakes will hinge on the preoccupations of that age group – friendships may be destroyed, individuality might be obliterated. There might be coming-of-age ordeals that the protagonists both welcome and fear. In a literary novel, the stakes may be personal values that seem to reflect something universal for the audience.

But whatever the conflicts are, make sure we understand why they are important and unavoidable.

Conflict begins at home

Conflict is not just good guys versus bad guys. It doesn't come only from your antagonists. In any situation that's dangerous or troublesome, there will be people on the same side who clash and make it far more messy.

In *Lord of the Flies*, the group of schoolchildren have the practical problems of survival, but these soon become much worse because of the personalities of the children. Each phase of the plot produces new challenges to each character's sense of right and wrong and their personal coping thresholds. It's conflict all the way, and yet they started off 'on the same side'.

If you put characters in a situation that causes trouble, each of them will react differently. They don't always have to turn traitor or become deadly enemies, but they won't all comply with full obedience to the story's mission. Teams of detectives, or scientists, or astronauts, or friends on holiday will all have their personal ways to tackle a problem, and as it becomes more desperate there will be rifts and disagreements. It's human nature to think you know better than somebody else, to fight about what's important, to form loyalties and rivalries – doubly so if the situation is unfamiliar or very challenging. It could even make for far more complications than the original problem.

If you have a bunch of characters on the same side, how could they tear each other apart?

Different views are there but they don't turn into action

So you have your characters with their different, individual opinions. But does anything happen because of them?

Lord of the Flies would be an insipid read if the characters held discussions about the rights and wrongs – and never did anything. But I see this in a lot of manuscripts.

Sometimes writers dig up these conflicts and put them into the characters' dialogue, but fail to translate them into action. Although it's plausible that some characters will talk a good fight and never act, and it's certainly true of polite society, it's disappointing in a story.

Stories must push characters so hard that they break the rules of politeness. These loyalties, interests, beliefs and opinions can't stay as theoretical conversation topics. They must be turned into struggles and dilemmas. The characters must be forced to make choices, to side with one person instead of another, to do what they feel is right and prevent what they feel is wrong. Or they must save their own skins, take the line of least resistance, make a ghastly compromise or act in spite or revenge. Or they must mess up completely because they don't know what to do. This is how a story takes us to an exciting place. If it doesn't, it means the characters are not being tested far enough.

If readers sniff a conflict, they anticipate it will escalate into action and tangible difficulties. They do not want it kept contained in thinking-sessions, discussions or musings by the narrative voice.

However, this doesn't mean the conflicts can't be expressed in dialogue, provided the dialogue becomes personal and wounding. Characters can say devastating things that will change their relationship irrevocably, like in *Who's Afraid of Virginia Woolf* – a vicious war between a married couple conducted mostly in the dialogue. The mistake is to make the dialogue a preparation for war – and never to fire a real weapon.

Push characters to the point where their conflicting views make them take action.

For your toolbox

- Open your eyes to opportunities for conflict.
- Make sure we understand why the conflicts are important and unavoidable.
- If you have a bunch of characters on the same side, how could they tear each other apart?
- Push characters to the point where their conflicting views make them take action.

5 Back story: before I tell you that, I'll explain this...

Back story is events that have happened before the narrative starts. Most stories have it, because they rarely start from the beginning of a character's life. However, 'back story' has become one of those phrases that critiquers mutter while grabbing the red pen – because writers tend to misuse it or include too much.

There are two fundamentals with back story.

The first is how to present it – a vivid flashback, a framed narration, a description of character background, a passage of exposition, a secret revelation that will change characters' feelings?

The second question is whether those events should be back story – or used as part of the main plot.

Most engaging events are buried in summary of back story

Do you know Donna Tartt's *The Secret History*? It starts with a murder. Then it winds back, and the first half of the book is a long flashback that tells how the main character, Richard Papen, met a group of exciting bohemian people, and eventually they murder their friend Bunny on a bleak, cold morning.

But another option might have been to come into the story at the moment when Richard discovers about the murder and leave him with this awful problem. His friends, who he idolises, have killed somebody. What will he do?

However, that would be leaving some of the most powerful, involving events as back story.

The murder of Bunny in *The Secret History* is dreadful, but not just because it's murder. It's because Richard has given his soul to these people – and we have shared that journey during the long flashback. If the development of the friendship had been left as background (the book's structure makes it easy to consider this question), we lose so much – the close connection with Richard, with the emotions and hopes he has invested in his exotic friends.

When we experience story events – either in real time, flashback, vivid recollection or some other device that plugs us into the character's consciousness – it becomes our own experience. In *The Secret History*, this experience is what gives Bunny's murder its power and makes the subsequent events so agonising.

I often see manuscripts where the writer has invented a

detailed and dramatic back story for a character, but the main story events lack impact and substance. There is no meat left for the book's real-time plot and so the novel seems empty and static. Of course, the story may be precisely that; the character might be coming to terms with past mistakes. The focus might be the finer detail of living with a burden, or leaving behind a golden period that is gone for ever. But just as often, this approach is not deliberate and the writer is scrabbling around, trying to find stuff for the characters to do. They don't realise they've already got fantastic ideas, but hidden them in the back story.

Could they be used as a fully fleshed flashback so the reader could participate? Or, more radically, could those same ideas be extracted from the past and reworked as the forwards plot? And what about the minor characters? Do they have back story events that are too good to keep *sotto voce*? What if they were given to a major player we should root for?

Often we're misled because of the way these ideas first arrive. We get a brainwave when we're thinking about a character's background, and then assume it must stay in the distance. The playwright, novelist and screenwriter Alan Bennett described in an interview how his best ideas are the ones that seem 'glimpsed out of the corner of an eye'. Experienced writers know this, and they know to examine every glimmer.

Consider whether your back story ideas should be front story.

Back story and secret wounds used instead of character development

Writers often try to get us interested in a character by giving them a colourful past. So the heroine was brought up by theatre folk, which the writer hopes will make her intriguing. It does, to a point, but it's only the start. The real value is in what this history has made of her. Does she crave security and a settled life as a result, or has it left her with itchy feet? Perhaps these twin urges are at odds inside her, sometimes pulling her one way, sometimes the other. What kind of people does she seek as friends? Is she more comfortable with those who are unconventional and bohemian, or does she prefer home-centred people who feel connected to mainstream society and the community?

The back story on its own is not enough to create a character. We must see how it has steered their choices. Also, back story works best if it exerts an active influence on the characters and plot events.

A variation of this back story problem is when a writer uses a past tragedy to get sympathy for their good guys – the secret wound. So a writer describes how a couple had a heartbreaking experience with fertility treatment many years before, or maybe their son was murdered. Although these ordeals are heartrending, and might make us feel for the couple, they don't in themselves show us the characters' natures. Fertility troubles and murder can happen to the worst of us too. Back story is a springboard for characterisation, not a substitute.

Still worse is the idea (derived from movies, which must streamline their stories) that a character is explained or decoded by a single key event in the past. Characterisation in prose doesn't generally work in one-shot doses or shorthand.

Individuality is not the colourful childhood or the horrifying event in the past. Individuality is how it formed them. Two people could have identical back stories, but react in opposite ways. One might witness his parents being killed by criminals and become a barely sane crimefighter known as Batman. Another might grow up to found an orphanage.

If an unusual origin or past traumatic event is key to how your character behaves now, don't forget to show us those consequences.

Dramatic issues and secret wounds are never used in the story

Many writers give their characters an exciting secret burden – which never features in the story. So they draw attention to their protagonist's long-lost brother, or mother whose identity was never known, or hidden romantic obsession, or puzzling birthmark – and nothing comes of it.

Such exciting character tidbits are like Chekhov's gun. If you load a firearm in the first act, the reader assumes it will appear later on. If not, you've teased them on false pretences – which will be noticed.

If you give your characters these colourful issues, do they have to be resolved? Not necessarily. Chekhov's gun doesn't have to be fired. Stories don't have to mete out rewards and answers in a simplistic way. The characters don't have to conquer every fear, or heal every injury. But each secret wound adds a tension, a marker that the reader watches for. It must colour the story in some way. It shouldn't be used only to grab interest and then disappear.

Sometimes the writer chooses not to delve further because they're hoping the reader will intuit what the secret wound means. But the reader can't, because the meaning will be different for each character – as we've been discussing with reactions to back story events. Suppose your character has a secret unrequited love. Although everyone can guess what this is like, they want to see what your characters feel and do. It's the reason they're curious. They don't want to generalise, they want to nose into the private life of the person it is happening to.

If your characters have secret wounds, make sure you explore them.

Back story in one major chunk at the beginning

The beginning of a novel is like starting an immense machine. The reader needs to know what's going on, who wants what, why it matters, who the characters are, what their relationships are, what they do day by day. It's easy to overload or confuse – and one of the common mistakes is to tell the back story too soon.

This wasn't always a problem. In the past, readers weren't so hungry for immediacy or the personal experience, so would accommodate a long tranche of back story as they settled in. Mervyn Peake's *Titus Groan* begins with detailed introductions to the setting and his characters before he ever puts them in situations where significant trouble is brewing. This certainly has its own virtues as, knowing the characters intimately, we are riveted when the major events happen. But a slow preamble can fatigue modern readers. If you're going to start with a lengthy introduction, for goodness' sake have a convict leap out from behind a gravestone on page one. Or push Bunny into a chasm.

If you look at the opening of a recently published well-edited novel, there is usually very little back story – just the minimum needed to establish context. And it's always related to the action in the scene.

So how much back story is enough at the start? It helps to relate this problem to real life. Imagine you have a new acquaintance. Certain things draw you together, help you get your bearings with the other person's personality, values and life. If the time comes to exchange your life histories, it will be after your relationship is established, when you are actively curious.

In the same way, the reader at the start of a novel can coast with a few well-deployed details – just enough to understand what's going on. The detailed picture might not emerge for a long time.

In *The Painted Veil* by William Somerset Maugham, we begin with a pair of lovers, Kitty and Townsend, who are nearly caught by Kitty's husband. There is much to know, especially about Kitty, the cheating, discontented wife. But Somerset Maugham doesn't begin with a lengthy introduction to her, or the ways she justifies her infidelity. First we see her in a moment of panic. This makes us curious about her as a person in a situation that scares her. Then he can spool out the back story whenever it's needed to give context to the events of the book. (There's more on beginnings – and this particular opening – in a dedicated section later.)

Back story is usually a lull. It tends to stop the forward momentum of the story. You have to judge when the reader is sufficiently hooked that this will not matter. Also, back story can often be served in small doses. In *Fahrenheit 451*, Ray Bradbury has a complex world to explain, which he plays out gradually. First, we get the bare bones – the protagonist Montag is at work, burning books. Then he is on his way home, and we get a little more detail, because Bradbury has made us curious about Montag's bizarre and disturbing job. Much later, the firemen witness a distressing suicide, and their captain gives them a pep talk to put them back on track. This is effectively explaining the world (exposition), but the characters have a need to hear it. In the next sequence, Montag is given a more detailed pep talk – which allows the captain to talk about some of the society's deeper issues. It's exposition again – but justified by the story.

Indeed, back story needn't be passive. It could create a bond between the characters or add drama.

In *Fahrenheit 451*, the captain's speech to Montag is more than just explanation. There's an undercurrent of menace as the captain is assessing Montag's reactions. The reader knows that Montag has hidden a few books in the apartment, which is strictly forbidden, and we wonder if they will be discovered. Just to make it worse, while the captain is there, Montag's wife discovers one of the books and cannot conceal her surprise. Has the captain has noticed, or is he turning a blind eye and giving Montag another chance? We don't know. So while the captain is explaining the world, we're aware of many tensions and questions. We're also learning about the characters, and Captain Beatty's relationship with Montag.

This scene has so much going on, under what appears to be an explanation of the world.

Effective writing often mirrors principles from real life. At the beginning, your book is forging a relationship with the reader, wooing them to bond with your characters and your persona on the page. There will come a point where your back story is very welcome. Indeed it doesn't have to be a lull. It might be very dynamic indeed.

Try to leave any major explanations of back story as late as possible.

Not all your back story is needed in the novel

The reader doesn't need to know every last note of the characters' pasts. Often, much of your back story is for you alone; it makes the characters and their dramas solid and helps you write with confidence.

Some writers make a draft that includes all the background – for their eyes only. Then they start a fresh file and fillet out everything that isn't current, looking for places to reintroduce context if needed. They find there is a lot that stays in the vaults.

Some writers limber up by writing back story up until the story starts, then delete it from the final narrative.

It's worth doing an editing pass to look for back story. Highlight anything that's explanation. Consider whether you could save it for later or give it a different use. Or even, if it could be taken out.

A rich back story helps you to write, but the reader may never need to see it.

Flashbacks

Flashbacks are undoubtedly useful. We might need scenes from a character's childhood, past relationships, or the week before the narrative began. But the difficulty with flashbacks is this: the present action isn't usually affected. A flashback doesn't change anything in the world of the story.

While back story can be used to cause change, for instance, if it's told in dialogue to another character, flashbacks might seem too static because they don't advance anything. However, they do add to our understanding, which is important.

That said, flashbacks can be more than simple explanation.

In *Something Like Normal* by Trish Doller, a teenage marine has returned home after a posting in Afghanistan. The current action of the story is his battle with post-traumatic stress disorder, his romance with a former classmate, and his return to normal life. Flashbacks to the warzone add an emotional punch, deepen our connection with him and lead us to root for his recovery.

Flashbacks might be pivotal in a story about memory. Angie Smibert's *Memento Nora* features a violent world where people can erase traumatic memories by taking a pill. But two characters decide that their memories must be preserved, and make them into a graphic novel, which sets off a disastrous chain of events. The flashbacks not only reveal dramatic events, they serve as a talisman for the novel's concerns – the value of remembering.

Like back story, flashbacks are best used when you've got the reader hooked enough to permit a trip to the past. If you venture backwards too soon, you might stall the story.

Make sure, if you use them, that we don't get the flashback confused with the main timeline. We must know where it starts and ends. If the flashback is long enough, it might be best as a section by itself or a whole chapter. If it's only a couple of paragraphs, make the transitions clear with your use of tenses. Use past perfect to make the switch and again to switch out – eg

> Harry drove through the dark lanes.

(Imperfect tense, in the story's current timeline.)

> It made him think of last summer, when Helena's daughter had gone missing.

(Past perfect, beginning of flashback.)

> For a brief period, all the village was united by the task

to find her. Warring neighbours walked side by side through the thick forest, scanning the ground for a torn scrap of her dress, a print from her shoe. Divorcing couples drove the countryside together in a spirit of co-operation, obeying the map without question, exploring every shed and shack. Henry and Angela were among them. It was a special, becalmed time, like a test whose reward would be another chance. The girl was found by their neighbour's son, with two broken ankles having jumped off the roof of a cowshed. Her survival, alas, hadn't mended his marriage.

(Past perfect again as we exit the flashback).

Now here he was, back in these dark woods...

Notice that I didn't use past perfect all the way through the flashback, because it's not as smooth to read. A sentence in past perfect at the beginning and end is enough to ease the reader in and out.

Connecting the flashback to a trigger works well too, such as a location that's been significant in the past, or an item found while clearing out the attic. It also gives you natural way to rejoin the present action when the flashback is over. Another route might be to introduce the flashback material in a dialogue scene, then break to a full flashback, and glide out again to your characters, still sitting by the fireside.

Flashbacks are easier to handle in first person or close third, as we're following the narrator's consciousness. If you're writing in omniscient third person, the narrative voice is more filmic. The transitions between current action and the past have to be marked more clearly.

Flashbacks can disturb the story's momentum, so include them once you've stoked the reader's curiosity. Also, make sure they are signposted clearly – unless you deliberately aim to create confusion.

Be gentlemanly with your research

In an earlier section, I talked about creating plots from special settings and jobs. This might require you to explain a lot of background. To complicate matters, half your readers might be experts already, which is why they chose your book.

So I'll say two words to you: hedge funds.

No, come back. Because Robert Harris set *The Fear Index* in the world of hedge funds – and explains it in a way that pleases both expert and newcomer.

He starts with characters in a situation we can relate to – a man with a mysterious intruder in his house. A good half of the book passes before the reader ever has to grapple with how a hedge fund works, though we understand it's important. The explanation comes as a flashback to the party where the main characters met, and because we're interested in them we want to read it. A racy rogue is trying to impress an introverted scientist – by explaining that hedge funds are like betting on whether the girl beside the fridge is wearing black underwear.

If you know about hedge funds, this is such fun that you forgive the simplistic explanation. If you don't, you emerge wiser. And the explanation never gets in the way of our stronger interest – how the characters met.

I see a lot of novels that handle research ineptly, with screeds of scene-setting exposition or unnatural dialogue. Instead, you want to knit the information into the story's life.

You don't want the reader confused, but it's easy to overdo insider details. Harris understands that however heavily he has to research, the novel should wear it lightly. His other thrillers tackle ancient Rome (*Imperium, Pompeii, Lustrum*), the 1940s wartime code-breaking centre Bletchley Park (*Enigma*) nineteenth-century French politics (*An Officer and a Spy*) to name but a few. They are full of intricate world-building, but he uses it sparingly, and translates it into conflicts that generate stories. Though it's economical, you never feel you're struggling to understand, or patronised by an oversimplification.

In your handling of research you have to be like the definition of a gentleman – a man who knows how to play the banjo but refrains from doing so. Know your world in depth, but wear your research lightly – put the story and characters first.

For your toolbox

- Consider whether your back story ideas should be the main story or a subplot.
- If you feel an unusual origin or past traumatic event is key to how your character behaves now, don't forget to show those consequences.
- Character is not the colourful childhood or the horrifying event. Character is how it formed them.
- If your characters have secret wounds, make sure you explore them.
- Leave the major chunks of back story as late as possible.
- A rich back story helps you to write, but the reader may never need to see it.

- Instead of cramming back story in at the beginning, reveal it as tantalising nuggets, or once the reader is desperate to know.
- Back story can do double duty – if characters reveal significant events to each other, it can deepen their bond.
- Flashbacks can disturb the story's momentum, so include them once you've stoked the reader's curiosity. Also, make sure they are signposted clearly – unless you deliberately aim to create confusion.
- Know your world in depth, but wear your research lightly – put the story and characters first.

6 What's happening?
And is it gripping?

Some stories keep us captivated with every scene. Others have plenty of developments but don't grab us. So it's not enough to show change or events. Here's what might be missing.

Events are dramatic but they don't seem to matter

A writer I was editing created a scene where Peter, a character we hardly know, loses his job. The sequence is presented without emotion or reaction from Peter, and the writer hopes we will intuit that it is bad news. Instead, it is dead on the page. Why?

Without knowing the character, we cannot appreciate the impact of this event. What plans will have to change, what are his immediate thoughts and who else might be affected? Is he worried about his family? Might he, for instance, have to keep up payments on the flat he has bought for his mistress? Are there gangsters who will break his legs for not paying their protection fees?

An event on its own is just a note on the page. A dry fact. It's empty unless we see the consequences.

But, you might argue, being fired is generally bad, right? I've seen many writers who hoped they could leave the reaction to the reader's imagination.

In some ways they are right. We don't want to spoonfeed or be obvious. What's more, filling the gaps makes readers knit themselves into the story more. The writer hopes we will intuit Peter's distress, become concerned for him and eager to know what he'll do. All of this will bond us more to the book – but only if we already know about Peter, or if we get to know him afterwards. (That wasn't what this writer did.)

If we've seen that Peter's got medical bills or needs to have his son privately tutored, or that he's being shafted by a sneaky colleague he once defended, the reader will have dots to join and emotions to feel. And so an event becomes a blow with impact. But without context, we don't know what being fired might mean to Peter and we can't supply this ourselves. For all we know, he might relish the freedom – we have no idea.

Here's another example. An accountant finds a dead body in the office store room. The writer shows us no reaction, in this scene or the next time we're with the character. This looks strange.

If there is no reaction, the reader interprets it as a deliberate message. Is it a clue that the accountant is not as mousy as she seems? Does this happen all the time? Did she grow up in a funeral home? Usually, though, the writer intends the character to be shocked – and has assumed we don't need to see it, ever. But you can see the chaos that arises in the reader's mind.

The writer usually has reasonable logic. Perhaps an upset reaction is too predictable, or would be uninteresting for the readership. If so, you could deal with it quickly. Describe how the accountant gasps when she makes the discovery and cut away swiftly. Or show her being comforted in a quiet corner as the detectives arrive. But if you don't acknowledge her response at all, the reader will draw quite the wrong conclusions. Don't forget to show a reaction if the characters are shocked.

No event has an automatic impact. The punch comes from context and consequence. If you begin a novel with news of a death, we are waiting to discover if this is disaster or welcome release. We're in your hands. We read on to find out which it is and whose life will be changed.

In section 4 I talked about conflict and stakes. Even the smallest decision a character makes can carry great peril – and drama – if it is presented the right way. Think of Winston Smith opening a book and writing his diary in it. It is a tiny action, with immense risk because of the context.

It's not the earthquakes that make the story, it's the shock-waves, the buildings that are smashed and the lives that are disrupted. An event will not be dramatic unless you show the drama it creates.

And if we let the reader fill the blanks, it can't be with generalisations. There is no such thing as a 'general' or 'typical' main character. There are distinct people who have their unique problems. Being fired isn't the point. The real point is what it did to Peter, his family, his secret life if he had one, his self-esteem, his plans, his friendships.

No event is dramatic in itself. Make us feel how it matters.

Instant breakdown after a shock or bereavement

From one extreme to the other – can a reaction to shock seem overdone? Yes it can.

When people receive shocking news or witness a dreadful incident, they do not usually accept or understand it immediately. They react with disbelief. A true shock is impossible to take in. The real impact is usually felt later.

I see this particularly when characters are told about the surprise death of a loved one. The writer has them instantly accept what has happened. They dissolve, poor things, into sobbing and anguish, perhaps declaring 'I can't believe he's gone'. This strikes the reader as off because it isn't true to life. Such news needs to sink in.

But if you replace the tears or outbursts with shock, denial or disbelief, it will work much better. If the character was much loved by the reader, this will also keep pace with their emotions because they may be reeling too. True grief will creep in later.

If your people have witnessed a horrifying accident they might react on a visceral level, scream hysterically to make it go away or attract help. This is an animal state; non-rational. They might do likewise if they are being shot at or threatened and have not had to handle such situations before. The dawn of understanding – and the expression of shock – will come more slowly.

When characters get tragic news or a shock, allow them disbelief and denial before they unleash their grief.

Dramatic act of self-sabotage not properly seeded

A good story has many slips between cup and lip, and sometimes a writer decides a character must destroy the thing dearly want. So they leave their lover, quit the precious job or refuse the scholarship.

The unexpected turn certainly has impact, indeed can be a shattering crisis if well handled. But it can just as easily seem implausible – or an arbitrary act of martyrdom invented by a writer who is scrabbling for a new story twist. Why is this?

Because the decision looks random unless certain foundations are laid. Although it should be a surprise, it should also make ghastly sense – if not at the time, soon afterwards.

Think of Jane Eyre, who leaves Mr Rochester when she discovers he already has a wife. This breaks our hearts but it isn't a sudden decision. Indeed it began long before the day on which Rochester's secret is revealed. For much of the relationship, we have seen Jane resist him because she feels precarious. In her world, servant lovers are easily discarded. Rochester has had to gain her trust and assure her they will have a legitimate life together. When it turns out he cannot marry her, we know how desperately this matters. She leaves. Her departure looks sudden, yet it makes awful sense. It's also extremely powerful because we have shared the deepening bond – which is then ruined. If this context had not been laid, Jane would look insane and would lose the reader's empathy.

How do we lay these foundations? They have to nest deep in the character. Perhaps we will see a flaw in their self-confidence; a secret that means they're living a lie; a situation of strain that cannot continue; a new development elsewhere that creates an intolerable conflict. With hindsight, the reader must see that the pressures have been gathering and so this tragic move is inevitable. (Either that or the cause of the turnaround should become a main mystery in the story – why would a person do something so apparently dumb?)

Sometimes when a writer fails with a twist like this they tell me they hoped the reader would guess the reasons. But actually, as we've seen with reactions to significant plot events, some blanks are too big for the reader to fill. The clues must be carefully placed.

Sometimes the writer hasn't even thought about the reasons, but knew by gut feeling that the development felt right. So they next need to consider how to make it arise naturally. Good plot twists are unexpected, but they also make sense. If they don't, the reader loses faith.

If your main character apparently torpedoes their own happiness, make us understand how they came to this sorry decision.

Nothing happens except conversations

Ivy Compton-Burnett wrote novels that consisted mainly of conversations, encouraging the reader to cast their own interpretation on the characters' dialogue. It's like reading a play; an incomplete, narrowed world where the reader has to seek the underlying nuances and fill the sparse information with insights of their own. That can sometimes be rewarding. Equally, many people find Ivy unreadable.

Quite a few writers give me manuscripts where most of the action is conversations. It reads like a radio play, with talk-scene after talk-scene.

This technique can be ideal if the narrowing effect is deliberate. A sequence of interviews, confessions, meetings or letters can create a fascinating story, and a reason why there might be tantalising blanks, too. But just as often, writers do this accidentally.

In *Writing Characters Who'll Keep Readers Captivated*, I talked about the opposite problem: manuscripts that are solid narrative, with hardly any dialogue. This creates a muted effect, like seeing characters through a filter. Again, there are style reasons to do this, but often it isn't a deliberate choice; the writer gets locked into their narrative mindset and can't let the characters wake up and speak. And the same happens the other way – the writer gets the characters talking and becomes stuck in that mode. When scenes happen that need to show action, they are locked in the groove of talk, and so they have the characters describe it to us.

If you're aiming for a natural effect, you need a balance. Characters must speak and they also must act. It is tricky to do both well and often impossible in one writing session. Many authors write or revise the dialogue sections in one pass, take a break and tackle the narrative elements another time.

If you find you can't imagine a scene except as dialogue, return to rewrite it again on a different day.

All the action follows a predictable path

At the start of a novel, we set up expectations. And some manuscripts deliver them with no surprises. The characters complete one step, then another – and plod onwards until the end.

This can be like reading the syllabus for an education course, or an account in a school magazine of the class trip to Stonehenge. There might be wrinkles that provide moments of humour or minor surprises, but there is an overriding sense that the milestones are passed, the goal is near, the assignment is being completed.

In a story, that looks dead dull.

Of course, your concept may dictate that the characters must reach their destination – if they're taking a trip on the Orient Express, flying to the Moon or growing up to become queen. If we know where they are heading, how do you surprise the reader?

The mistake is to fixate on the goal, the destination. The story is not the destination. The story is the journey. Find the ways in which it was not ordinary or conventional.

Create situations that will challenge the individual characters and split the loyalties of the group. Have war break out, so that the goal takes on a new significance. Play with the characters' commitment level. The keenest enthusiasts might grow to hate the mission. The cynical naysayer might throw their heart in by the end. When they get to the Moon or the throne, it was the ride of their lives.

Compare this with the syllabus outline. The goal is achieved, the steps are completed, but there is no sense of transformation. (There could be, though, if the experience was written with that in mind.)

Here's an example. It isn't literary, but it rocks the goal-oriented story. In the 2000s Channel 4 in the UK had a reality TV series *Faking It*. It was conceived as a modern-day *Pygmalion*, where ordinary people were coached to pass themselves off in a world they had no experience of. *Faking It* appears to offer a predictable plot – rookie has to follow a syllabus, acquire expertise and pass a test. Except the real story was their emotional journey.

First, the new world challenged the participants' social and cultural values, often promising a hilarious mismatch. A tweedy fine art student had to pass as a streetwise graffiti artist. A classical cellist had to become a nightclub DJ. A laddish sailor would be turned into a drag queen.

Sometimes the participant assumed the task would be a breeze. Surely it couldn't be hard to spin records in a nightclub if you could play Elgar on the cello? They might feel superior to their tutors. What could be so demanding about scrawling on a wall with spray paint? Often the mentors viewed their charges with similar disdain. The characters were set for an interesting clash.

To successfully fake, these barriers had to go on both sides. Respect had to grow. Then the faker had to dig for a personality that suited the new world. The cellist had to lose her inhibitions. The art student had to discover a genuine gritty confidence where he could hold his own with expressive people.

The test day arrived, as we expected, but it was never predictable. It was no longer about fooling judges or winning a bet. It was about passing a test in personal liberation – a new and more complete way to live.

Indeed, *Faking It* follows the classic hero's journey plot or monomyth, as described by Joseph Campbell. The character embarks on a challenge and assumes it will be easy. While they settle in, it's fun or trivial. Then they become committed and start to worry that they won't succeed. Finally they return, changed. This pattern doesn't fit every story, by any means, but it certainly fits *Faking It*.

I'll say it again: the story is not about the result, or reaching the destination. The story is the difficulty of getting there and the chronicle of change.

Indeed, most stories create expectations about the final destination. They plant an element that, when fulfilled, will make it feel properly completed. Sherlock Holmes has to solve the mystery. Susie Salmon, the murdered girl in Alice Sebold's *The Lovely Bones*, has to see justice done. Flora Poste in *Cold Comfort Farm* has to find a new home. The characters are heading there, inch by inch, but their route can be as fractal and loopy as you like.

If the final destination of your story is obvious, make the journey one of epic change.

The 'you are here' scene and other smart ways with plot exposition

If you're old enough to remember the TV series *Charlie's Angels*, there was always a scene where the feisty gals recapped everything they knew about the week's case. This was usually half-way through. Although it sounds formulaic when described like that, viewers were probably grateful. In a complicated plot with lots of twists, turns and red herrings, it's useful to give the reader a 'you are here' moment, with a recap of what's been learned and what the stakes are.

Also, the 'you are here' scene can provide a welcome breather from the hurly-burly – especially if most of the book is breathlessly tense. Even in fast-paced genres, readers can only take so much before they long for a lull where everyone can relax. (I'll come back to this later in the section on pacing, p126.)

So here are some stylish ways to use the 'you are here' scene.

Develop a relationship This is a fine example from a manuscript I critiqued. Two characters in a dangerous investigation were thrown into prison. With nothing else to do, they began the 'you are here' discussion. As they talked, we began to be aware of a growing attraction between them. On one level, it was good to get the recap of the current problems and what they feared might happen. But also, we were riveted by how they reacted to each other.

You could also use the 'you are here' moment as an opportunity for characters to offer trust or friendship, especially if they have been at loggerheads before.

Plant seeds obliquely and echo a character's central trouble In *Strong Poison* by Dorothy L Sayers, Lord Peter Wimsey is trying to clear Harriet Vane of murder. Half-way through, he reluctantly visits his family for Christmas and they gossip about the notorious Harriet, as the case is a national outrage. Wimsey finds their conversation distasteful, so while we get the recap, we also see his reactions, which tell us about his growing feelings. The family also talk about another family member who is – scandalously – marrying a Jewish girl, which draws our attention to love across boundaries. This in turn plants the seeds for Wimsey's ultimate proposal to Harriet.

Create a dilemma If you need a 'you are here' scene and the character has nobody to talk to, turn it into a dilemma. Make your character ruminate over the clues they have and wonder what to do. In Eric Ambler's *The Mask of Dimitrios*, a mystery writer becomes obsessed with a murdered criminal. He deliberates whether to continue with his search or to take the sensible option and go home to his quiet life (and finish writing his book). In doing this, Ambler involves us as his character thinks through the case, discards the sensible path and commits to the foolhardy but exciting one.

Split the info-dump to create mystery If you have to introduce a large tract of information, does it have to go into one scene? In some stories, a group of detectives interview informants or witnesses, who deliver lengthy lectures of explanation. This can be a lifeless read and tricky to remember.

Like back story, you might not have to deliver it in one go. Could you split it into smaller bites to provoke our curiosity? Indeed, it doesn't have to be static information. Could you work it into puzzles and mysteries, give the characters tantalising leads to follow? If so, congratulations. You just generated more momentum for your plot.

If you have to include an exposition scene, find a way to make it perform another story function as well.

Mystery – writer doesn't play fair with secrets

Stories thrive on mysteries and twists. Of course they do. But sometimes writers use underhand tactics to create them.

For instance, we have a character whose thoughts and feelings we have been sharing. He writes an email. The writer doesn't tell us what it says, which strikes the reader as jarringly vague, as so far we've been privy to the character's full experience. Indeed, if he's written anything else, we've seen it – texts, birthday cards, notes to the milkman. But we don't see this email. Then, a few chapters later, the email upsets another important character, which is a plot surprise. At that point its text is revealed to the reader – and it's clear that if we had seen it when it was sent, the coming backlash would have been obvious. The email has been concealed so that the writer could spring this plot surprise.

Most of us would think that wasn't playing fair.

A narrative builds a code of conduct. It establishes whether the narrator is reliable or unreliable, self-aware or in denial. By the time we're done with the first few chapters, a grammar is formed. We understand what the characters will share with the reader – including how selective their memory is. When you change that level of disclosure, the reader notices. If you do it unfairly to spring a plot twist or other surprise, it jolts us out of the story world.

I've seen this inconsistent censoring principle work in many sneaky ways. In one manuscript, a writer revealed – on page 201 – that a viewpoint character had been receiving blackmail letters for a year. We had seen everything else the character cared about, but not this. The writer hid it because he wanted to save it as a surprise.

Here's another example. We're told that our protagonist Dr Shaw does scientific research. When the other characters discover its nature late into the story, it causes mayhem because Dr Shaw is researching something that is morally unacceptable to them. However, this secret has been kept from the reader too, in an unfair way because it has broken the grammar of the narrative. We have been following Dr Shaw's life as close confidante, fully aware of everything she is doing. When she makes coffee, we see the kettle being filled, the beans being ground, the milk being steamed. Internal dialogue keeps us with her thoughts, and she notes she's using Columbia beans, skimmed milk. However, when she works in her lab, this disclosing style is withdrawn. She uses pipettes and looks down microscopes, but nothing she uses or observes has a name, despite the fact that she must be using it in her own mind as she does her work, just as she did when she made coffee. The science lab scenes are being shown through a veil of censorship that doesn't fit with the rest of the narrative. It's cheating for the sake of giving the reader a surprise.

Certainly some stories are told from a distanced perspective, which leaves room for the reader to deduce the truth. There's nothing wrong with that. It's consistent and fair. And you might make exciting effects if you deliberately veil parts of the narrative. Or perhaps the character will withdraw their confidential relationship with the reader, becoming unreliable or increasingly unwilling to share. Meanwhile the reader adds more from their intuition and knowledge of what has gone before, and becomes increasingly involved, and eager to find the truth. This is fair because it conforms to the narrative grammar.

And you can certainly use the veiling effect if it won't bust your story logic. Ruth Rendell does it in *The Keys to The Street*. One of the narrators is revealed to be another character's man of mystery. How does she do it? She writes in the close perspective of several different characters. One chapter is by Mary, another by Leslie and so on. Some characters know the mystery man and mention him by name. The characters who don't can plausibly describe him as a passing stranger because that is how they know him. Crucially, when the surprise is revealed, the reader doesn't feel it's contrived.

When you conceal a surprise, ensure you play fair by the narrative's rules.

Mystery – too little or too much?

Mysteries are such fun, whatever type of story you write. They encourage readers to examine evidence, ask questions, knit their minds into the book. But readers need rewards too – a motive uncovered, a secret friendship revealed – so they feel they are making progress.

Sometimes, writers save all the answers until the end. They seem afraid to reveal anything too quickly. Or perhaps they didn't solve the puzzles until they wrote the closing chapters.

A novel that gives no answers until the climax is a tough read. It's better to drip a revelation in, and let it pose a more delicious question. Intensify the mystery, make it deeper and wider than the reader first suspected. Misdirect; create more twists and near misses.

If you didn't solve the mysteries yourself until the end of your first draft, go back and stitch some reward scenes in. And don't try to skimp with an isolated line or two – that will hardly be noticed by the reader. Write scenes, show dialogue, make the characters act on this gained knowledge. This ensures the reader remembers it (show not tell).

You can also use little payoffs to vary the pace of the story. I'll talk about this later in its own section, but briefly, small successes let the reader breathe. They also allow the characters to look more capable, instead of mercilessly bullied by their impossible quest.

Although you should save your biggest reveals until the end, keep the reader motivated with rewards along the way.

Mysteries solved before you've got them started

Don't do the opposite and give the answers before you've got the reader interested. Sometimes writers rush their revelations. Or they haven't understood how to allow separate threads to develop in a tantalising way. Curiosity can't be hurried or forced.

When you answer a question, make sure you've primed the reader to ask it. Give them time to get intrigued.

So: you might reveal that the village veterinary surgeon is a drug dealer. You teased the reader with a line that said he had a mysterious second mobile phone. Did you give the reader enough time to wonder about that before you give them the answer? Did you make them wonder if he has a secret lover? Or if he is merely careless and disorganised?

Before you answer the mystery, did you make the most of the intrigue?

The power of choices

Here's a dramatic tale. A rock star had a seizure in his hotel room. He recalled little of it; just a long fight to breathe. As he regained consciousness, the other band members were telling the paramedics he'd be fine for the night's gig, a doctor would take care of him. He didn't want to let them down, of course, but he felt like death.

His girlfriend had witnessed the unremembered time: ten minutes of jerking, clawing and choking, pleading for help; the brutal rescue where paramedics only just got him back. She saw the other band members playing down the dangers, arguing with the medics. She wanted to tell them how bad he was before any of them arrived, and how long it went on for; except he was so fragile that might trip another attack. And none of the band would listen anyway.

Who is in the worse situation? The rock star or the girlfriend?

In real life the question would be idiotic. But in story terms, it's worse to be the girlfriend. Therefore, she's the character we're more interested in.

But many writers would make the rock star the central character.

Why is the girlfriend more fascinating to readers? She has the heavier burden. She knows that if she could muster enough guts, wits and nous, she could defy the band and save her lover. Her conscience is telling her so. But she is outnumbered, has no clout, and even the boyfriend will listen to them rather than her. She is trapped and isolated with her problem. And even if her boyfriend gets through this show, what about the next and the next? She is burdened with guilt and responsibility. He is burdened only with biology.

When writers want to make us concerned for a character they often try to enlist our sympathy with a trauma or a timebomb. But the reader knows the writer can use a timebomb as the whim takes them; either the rock star dies or doesn't. Choices and decisions, though, exploit what stories do best; they pit characters against each other, against their own failings, fears and weaknesses. In the above scenario, although the reader might be concerned for the rock star as a fellow human being, they'll really be gripped by the girlfriend.

Great stories make us walk in a character's emotions and wonder what they will do. A terrific way to do that is to give characters difficult choices. Can she stand up to these people? Does she have the courage to do the right thing? What would it kick off? Could that choice drive the plot forwards? Will she muster the ability to convince people of her point of view? Might she be thrown out of Eden, a point of no return? If she does the wrong thing, she carries it like a wound herself, but one that was made by the story and her own actions. We can feel this struggle, every step.

Use choices and dilemmas to create compelling story situations.

For your toolbox

🖎   No event is dramatic in itself. Make us feel how it matters.

🖎   When characters get tragic news or a shock, allow them a period of disbelief and denial before they unleash their grief

🖎   If your main character apparently torpedoes their own happiness, even if it is a surprise, make sure we understand how they came to this sorry decision.

🖎   If you find you can't imagine a scene except as dialogue, return to it and re-edit on a different day.

🖎   If the final destination of your story is obvious, make the journey one of epic change (hero's journey).

🖎   If you have to include an exposition scene, find a way to make it perform another story function as well.

🖎   When you conceal a surprise, ensure you play fair by the narrative's rules.

🖎   Although you should save your biggest reveals until the end of your novel, keep the reader motivated with rewards along the way.

🖎   Before you reveal the answer to a mystery, did you make the most of the intrigue?

🖎   Use choices and dilemmas to create compelling story situations.

7 When the reader stops believing: cliche, coincidence and convenience

Here's one of the paradoxes of story. Readers know that the writer is pulling the strings, deciding whether the car's brakes will fail or a character's bluff will work. One of your jobs is to enthral them so much they forget about this. And that means you have to avoid doing anything that wakes them from your spell.

Cliches, coincidence and convenience are real danger points. Cliches can remind the reader they've seen a phrase or a plot twist before and undermine the immediacy of the experience. Coincidences and convenient happenings remind the reader you can do whatever you want.

Here's where the hazards lurk and what to do about them.

Coincidence – the dos and don'ts

How many stories start with a coincidence? These are fine. Coincidences to start trouble are great. They're often the reason why you're telling the story. Coincidences beyond that point start to look suspiciously unimaginative or lazy. And coincidences to solve a crucial plot problem are best not attempted.

Its close cousin is convenience. Some authors make the plot elements fall into place too easily. The characters go into the market on the very day they will bump into the right people. Or a character goes to the solicitor to update her will and instead is – gosh – offered a job, which solves her problems at a stroke. The writer thought they were being casual and random, but it usually looks too contrived.

Of course, you want your characters in the right place at the right time, but you must make it look credible. If a character will bump into someone important, divert the reader's attention by sending them to the location for another purpose.

Make it look as though they were trying to avoid somebody, and then have them bump into somebody else – perhaps a person they owe money to. The sleight of hand will make the encounter a surprise. Or give them a different mission. Perhaps they'd broken a precious item and were desperate to find a replacement – and while the reader is concentrating on whether they find it, the important encounter happens. If the character will get the job at the solicitor, make them earn it – perhaps by helping the senior partner sort out a tech problem so that someone mentions the vacancy.

A coincidence that adds to the characters' problems is okay, though. But you can probably get away with it only once.

Any time a development looks convenient, try your darndest to make it a surprise.

Characters jump to correct conclusions or interview only the right people

This is a variation of the previous point, but worth a separate note. In some manuscripts I read, no one makes any wrong assumptions. There are no misunderstandings that send characters along the wrong path. If the characters are detectives they all have spot-on deductive skills and insight. If they need information, they will – so conveniently – find just the right person to ask.

This problem isn't confined only to crime novels. Almost any story might require characters to find information, objects, locations or people.

When characters get what they badly want, it should be earned. It's dull to read about people sifting clues and always getting the right answer. As I discussed in the section on predictable plots, the story is in the challenge. You need to convince us the characters might fail unless they are clever, courageous – or maybe outrageous.

You can have fun using the reader's expectations. Hint that the character is trying to solve the problem the wrong way, and make the reader mutter to themselves, 'don't do that, you're wasting time' or 'this can only end badly'. Or swivel it around. Pretend the plan is going well and turn it into a disaster.

You can also use the rule of three. Let your characters try two drastically wrong solutions before they hit on the right one.

If your characters need something important, make the search difficult for them.

Obstacle overcome too quickly

Characters shouldn't achieve their goals too easily, so we introduce obstacles. A detective is trying to assemble a squad to search a house, but can't call for backup. He has to risk tackling an armed murderer on his own. We read, our hearts in our mouths. But if a passing squad car came to the rescue, the reader might feel cheated because they were teased with a more exciting situation. (Unless you revisit the danger later, with the detective truly isolated.)

Beware of despatching your plot obstacles too easily. If you do, they're not obstacles. You can do it if it's fair, entertaining and surprising – but often it looks as though the writer was afraid to explore further, for fear of diverting the story or making it impossible to complete.

It's very disappointing if you introduce a conflict or obstacle, then fix it instantly and carry on as you were. These troubles are the story too, the most intriguing part.

Here's another example. I'll read a sentence that goes:

> Michael persuaded Sheena when the kids were born to
> give up her job in PR, and it was quite a struggle...

This is promising. It sets an alert: Michael and Sheena have tensions. But then –

> ... Thankfully it had never soured their relationship.

It was resolved so quickly? Why mention it at all? Isn't it more intriguing if Sheena resented giving up her job?

Indeed, it's more likely the reader will assume the statement about Michael and Sheena does not represent the absolute truth. It could be a sign that Michael hopes all is well and doesn't want to dig further. Or that Michael envies Sheena because he thinks she's fulfilled.

Often these ideas come to us as we're writing. We like them because they seem to add frisson or realism. But they weren't what we'd planned so we squash them. *Dear reader, you wonder if Sheena has complicated reactions to this, but let me assure you that everyone is perfectly harmonious. I put that idea in because it seemed more realistic but I don't want it to disrupt the story. Please forget about it now.*

But unbidden ideas are often worth exploring. Remember Alan Bennett glimpsing his best breakthroughs in the corner of his eye? These ideas are like yeast. They add richness, complications and life.

However, you might solve a conflict quickly and bring it back later.

So a plucky schoolgirl called Larissa finds herself alone and abandoned in a rough city. With no friends and no money, what will become of her? Unsavoury ruffians are eyeing her up. Then luckily, Larissa is found by her uncle and the threat recedes. But trouble has been promised, and was used to create jeopardy. If Larissa later has to confront it properly with no easy rescue, all well and good. If, however, it never returns, the reader was teased on false pretences.

Look for moments where you might have despatched a story obstacle too quickly.

Disasters and acts of God:
prime the reader with foreshadowing

Spoiler alert: *The Sea, The Sea,* Iris Murdoch

Readers have a strong sense of whether surprises are fair. Sudden fatal coronaries, floods, falling trees and brake failures have to be used with careful judgement because they are convenient for the writer.

They must be foreshadowed so that they seem inevitable and surprising but not arbitrary.

So why must the reader be primed for them? In real life we don't get warnings. Shocking events simply happen. But actually, if you look closer, we don't accept them that readily. Indeed, one of the first reactions is denial, to reject what's happening – as we've discussed in the earlier section about how characters react to devastating news.

In fiction, we don't want the reader to reject what's happening, not for a nanosecond. It breaks the spell. That's doubly undesirable if your disaster solves a problem or creates a twist. Of course, we still want the surprise.

So we prepare the reader with hidden clues, an atmosphere that makes the event more possible.

You can foreshadow specific events, such as a car crash. You could plant a hint much earlier in the novel that one of your characters is often fined for speeding, or that it's Christmas and drunk-drivers are on the roads.

Foreshadowing mustn't be obvious, so you need to disguise your intentions by making the scene appear to perform some other function – such as a couple arguing about who will stay sober for the drive home.

You could introduce a mini pre-disaster. Your victims might

hit a patch of ice while driving. They glance at each other urgently while the car glides impossibly sideways, then the tyres bite, the car becomes obedient and they carry on nattering. The safe world slipped away, but is restored – for now. Then later you can hit them big time.

Iris Murdoch uses the setting to foreshadow various accidents in *The Sea, The Sea*. Early in the book, the narrator moves to a house on the coast, and often mentions the difficulty of climbing up the slippery rocks. These are presented as part of the trials of his new environment, a shock after his smart pad in London. They also help us believe in the later catastrophes.

Another way to foreshadow a catastrophe is to give a character a moment of irrational fear. So our couple are saying farewell and the husband clings longer than usual, whispering 'be careful'. 'I'll be fine,' laughs the wife, and sweeps away through the boarding gates. Then we're prepared either for her plane to crash or – with a neat reversal – something to happen to him.

You could also use language and imagery that suggest a state of instability.

Charles Dickens and Charlotte Bronte use the weather as a device for pathetic fallacy, with storms echoing their protagonists' sense of unease or foreboding. This also seems to link their fortunes to something elemental and wild, so that the cruel twists seem somehow destined.

Often these acts of preparation are tiny, and slip past our notice because they fulfil another function – scene-setting or an echo of a character's state of mind. But they leave a trace of apprehension that stops a disaster looking arbitrary. Instead it becomes strangely fated and inevitable.

If disaster strikes, prepare the reader obliquely.

Same handy plot-changing event
happens to two separate people

Sometimes we don't realise we're repeating our clever plot developments. So in one chapter, a highly stressed middle-aged man slumps over his desk with a heart attack, which makes way for a talented junior. Then later in the same novel, another highly stressed middle-aged man collapses on the golf course, creating problems (or solutions) for all concerned.

The repetition could be significant, of course. The characters might have been poisoned. They might be twins with the same cardiac timebomb, or from a family with an atrocious record in heart health. Or perhaps the writer intends a comic effect of symmetry or natural justice. But it will not work if they are intended as two realistic, unrelated – and plot-changing – events.

But – you might say – the writer has used this repetition to establish that coronaries happen to stressed characters. But readers know that a lot of stressed executives don't have them.

This is a good point. In our stories we have to establish a set of world rules. But in the end, it comes down to the writer's intention. The more convenient the coronary is for the plot, the more respectfully it must be used. If it happens a second time, we must be aware that the reader will notice it – as a deliberate clue or the style of the world.

Beware of using the same plot-changing event twice without good reason.

Characters tread water until they save the day

In an earlier section I talked about situations where the writer loads the most interesting events into back story, leaving the characters with nothing to do in the real-time action of the book. This makes for a rather static read. I see this similar problem with peripheral and supporting characters.

These characters have lives that are curiously limited. We might see a lot of scenes where they have lunch with the main character, or leave phone messages. We might wonder why we're seeing them so frequently because their scenes are not especially interesting or revealing, and don't contribute to the story's progress. Neither do they offer useful insights from a trusted perspective or a barometer of change. It is conspicuous that they don't do anything – until the day they get a major character out of a hole. The lady who lunches can volunteer for a mad dash to hospital, or shoot the antagonist with a pistol.

This is a tricky generalisation, because there are instances where a cheeky surprise can work. But usually when characters twiddle their thumbs until their big moment it looks contrived. The reader notices that you had nothing important for them to do until then.

If a character will surprise us by saving the day, we should have a sense that they conduct a life of their own. Give them snippets of background action and independence before the rescue scene. Also, sew them into the story more. It's fine for them to have lunch all the time if those scenes also offer something else – a sense of deepening trust, an influence of sanity in an increasingly mad situation. Or you might even want to keep them down deliberately, always offering help but being refused for some delicious, complicated human reason. Let these characters contribute to the story before they have their heroic moment.

If a supporting character saves the day, make sure they have an important role in other ways.

Desperately seeking coincidences for a spectacular finish: *The Kite Runner*

Spoiler alert

We're constantly seeking to tie up threads, streamline our sprawl of ideas, reincorporate events and create coherence. But sometimes we can go too far. I find this with Khaled Hosseini's novel *The Kite Runner*.

The story begins with Amir and Hassan, two boys in Afghanistan. As a child, Amir overhears his father complaining he is a coward, and saying Hassan, the son of the servant, is the kind of brave son he wanted. One day Amir witnesses Hassan being raped and is too scared to help. After that, he is so ashamed he gradually destroys their friendship. Amir and his father flee Afghanistan for a new life in America. Fast forward and adult Amir gets a call from a family friend. Hassan is dead but has a son, who is now in an orphanage in Afghanistan. Amir makes the risky journey to rescue the child but finds he has been taken away by a Taleban warlord. He plunges into a world of real danger to find Hassan's child and rescue him.

The novel has many coincidences, which bother readers to a greater or lesser extent. Here I'm going to address the one that for me is most major – because it aims to be the climax of the story. What's more, the story would have worked without it.

Remember Hassan was raped? The rapist – that very same man – is now working for the Taleban warlord and satisfying his urges on Hassan junior. And Amir has to confront him. For me, this is where it unravels. There must have been thousands of men in Afghanistan who abuse little boys, and hundreds of warlords who would employ them. But Amir runs into this selfsame one. And the boy – of all possible boys he could have picked – is

Hassan's son. That's an impressive heap of coincidences. What are the odds?

What makes this extra annoying is that the story would work better without it. Amir does not need to confront that selfsame person. His real need is to let go of a situation that has haunted him all his life. He doesn't need a second chance with those people. He needs a second chance with himself. Indeed, it's not even necessary that the abused boy is Hassan's son. Amir could save any innocent from a violent man and it would do the same for him and for the story.

This is a curious use of coincidence. Most of the time, writers resort to it as an easy plot solution or to fix a problem they have made too impossible. This coincidence in *The Kite Runner* is intended to give a story a big emotional finish – but it doesn't because it's so hard to believe. In fact, the story won't fall apart without it; it would be stronger. I'll return to it in the section on endings as there's more to say.

If you're using a coincidence to create a big finish, make sure we will believe it.

Most story revelations come when a character blurts something out

In some manuscripts, the only significant revelations come when a character says something they shouldn't.

Unless it's a deliberate style choice – ie the novel is mostly dialogue – this looks artificial. But as we discussed earlier, it's easy to fall into this groove if you've got stuck in the mindset for writing dialogue.

This problem is also a key feature of a novel with a passive main character who doesn't do much on their own initiative. Instead of making discoveries, they get a handy, talkative visitor who delivers the next bombshell.

In a variation on this, the main revelations happen because characters make a verbal slip. There's nothing wrong with having one character who causes trouble because they are tactless, careless or catty. But to have several? You know what I'm going to say: it looks lazy.

Of course, some discoveries must come through conversations. So we need to find interesting ways to provoke them. Have a character stumble into a situation where something clandestine is going on, such as a tryst with a secret lover, and make them act on their suspicions. Let a character trick somebody into giving away a confidence. Or find a way to shift the discovery to a sequence of action – they could watch another character unseen or open somebody's mail.

Be careful how you use characters who blurt out important revelations. Don't rely on it as your only means of advancing the plot. Have characters make discoveries in other ways too.

A fight isn't enough – the reader knows you control the outcome

Fights are not as gripping in prose as writers imagine. Readers know the characters will trade blows or fire bullets until help arrives or someone falls over. So in stories, really good fights have to be won on something else. Especially at the climax.

What makes a satisfying end to a fight? It's usually a surprise. Perhaps it's a David and Goliath scenario – the little guy turns out to have bigger and better ideas than the beefy opponent. James

Bond, even though he's tough, can't defeat an ultimate foe with just a single gunshot. He has to use his wits as well.

Sleight of hand is good too, especially for characters who aren't fighters by profession or nature. A doctor could confiscate a bottle of moonshine from a patient earlier in the day, and use it as a handy impromptu weapon when he has to fight for his life. (Improvisation with objects is good in a physical fight – particularly if you use something that was forgotten about.) Perhaps the protagonist does something surprisingly brave – especially at the climax, when they might overcome a longstanding problem.

Prose is an internal medium. We are gripped far more by choices and dilemmas than we are by physical action and danger (as we saw in an earlier discussion). Prose is not like films and TV, where visual wham-bam physicality can be thrilling in its own right. Prose is much better for emotional action. A scene that is merely a set of physical instructions will never be as interesting as one with character interaction, humour, or a development that matters to one of the players. Indeed, screenwriter Jane Espenson said she found it hard to write the fights in *Buffy the Vampire Slayer*, so she would design the scene about something else – an argument or a revelation between the characters.

There's an interesting example of a gripping action sequence in Ray Bradbury's *Martian Chronicles*. A group of astronauts are hunting a deserter, Spender, who has shot several of his crewmates. The astronauts' captain, Wilder, has several opportunities to shoot Spender, but is reluctant, in spite of what Spender has done. Each time Wilder has Spender in his sights, he has the dilemma – does he shoot or not? For the good of the group, he should. But as a human, he wants to find a better solution. So every moment of the hunt vibrates with this tension.

This principle doesn't only apply to fights or physical combat. You can use it for any situation that requires a physical skill – defusing a bomb, tracking a killer through the woods. And if you can't think of a cunning way to add tension through the decisions, make it into a 'how-to' scene that the reader will be gripped by because it's so darn fascinating. So the character says

> Most bombs aren't defused by cutting a wire. You have to get inside the mind of the man who built it.

The reader will let you off if you keep them enthralled with interesting knowledge from the special world. You could also use it to tell an anecdote from the character's back story:

> I was there the day that Frank defused the bomb in the lift mechanism of the Empire State Building...

At the end of *The Empire Strikes Back* there is the famous showdown fight between Luke Skywalker and Darth Vader. There's a riot of lightsabres and grappling, but the moment everyone remembers is Vader's line:

> I am your father.

That's the killer.

Look for the emotional dimension in a fight or action scene, or make it into a 'how-to'.

Unavoidable plot events and devices

Many genres have obligatory scenes that could turn into cliche. Some of them are unavoidable as well, which creates an interesting challenge. Chick-lit usually finishes in a chase to stop the loved one being lost for good (usually at the airport). Thrillers have a scene where the detective or the agent confronts the serial killer or arch-villain. Whodunnits have the explanation. If they are not there in some form, the reader will feel cheated.

The mistake is to think there is nothing new you can do with the idea. This is a challenge to get creative.

All stories work by setting up expectations, and when you have a predictable element you have a pre-established mechanism for surprise.

You could prime the reader to anticipate a particular crisis, then take it somewhere else.

Suppose your people are marooned in the wilderness. Sooner or later, one of them will have a serious injury or illness that will be fatal without sophisticated medical help. Here are two ways that writers have taken it beyond the obvious.

Jose Saramago's *Blindness* is set in a world where the population is struck by a mysterious blinding contagion. The initial sufferers are imprisoned in an old mental hospital so they won't infect the rest of the world. One of the characters is injured and the wound becomes infected, but the authorities refuse to help. Finally, the character crawls to the perimeter, where a panicky guard shoots him. The soldier is representing the outside world, and his action speaks for the world's horror and fear.

Alex Garland's *The Beach* is set in a secret paradise island community, and one character (Christo) is seriously injured in a shark attack. The community leader forbids anyone to fetch help because it would reveal their existence to the world. They try to cope with Christo themselves, until he becomes so distressingly ill that they carry him to the middle of the jungle and leave him to die. This horrifying act is a focus point for the tensions in the group and the beginning of a great undoing.

Blindness and *The Beach* take the same well-worn plot situation – and treat it in startling ways.

When you use real historical or contemporary events, you face the same problem. The reader may already know what will happen – so the presentation and use of it is everything. In *Wolf Hall*, Hilary Mantel was dealing with the court of King Henry VIII. When Anne Boleyn goes into confinement to give birth, it's no surprise that she has a daughter (Elizabeth I) instead of the son that Henry hopes for, and that this will be her undoing. Mantel used that knowledge to potent effect. She describes a scene where Boleyn is taken by ceremonial barge to the palace in Greenwich, and the tender way she is treated because she carries the hopes of the nation. It is poignant as we feel how fragile and doomed she is.

If you have a plot event or story device that seems to be obligatory, find an unexpected way to use it.

Contrived conflicts and dumb plot moves

Spoiler alert: *Bel Canto*, Ann Patchett

We rely on obstacles to make a plot interesting and unpredictable. We use misunderstandings and mishaps to keep the principals apart in a romance. We lay red herrings and wrong turnings in a mystery. We show impulsive decisions in almost any kind of story. But these must be natural to the characters and situation.

I see a lot of pivotal plot actions and obstacles that look unconvincing because they are only possible if the characters become stupid or reckless. They brood over suspicions that would be sorted out if someone asked a common sense question. They embark on long investigations that could be cut short if somebody pursued a more obvious line of inquiry. They get into danger because the writer wants a particular showdown, when actually it is more likely they would wait for help or take proper precautions.

Sometimes writers keep the characters running around on a flimsy pretence of mystery. In *The Da Vinci Code*, the heroes seem unable to solve the simplest puzzles – because the plot needs them to chase around for clues, getting into danger. A moment's thought or a call to an expert would have given them the answers.

Of course, a good plot should put characters under uncommon stress. So they are likely to be rash, forgetful, flustered, unreasonable or paranoid. They might choose danger instead of safety. But we have to make sure the reader understands this. There's a scene near the end of Ann Patchett's *Bel Canto* where characters have the opportunity to walk away from the building where they are being kept hostage. They don't, because by this stage they are far more bonded to the world within the walls of the embassy. We'll accept that characters make unwise moves if we understand their emotional reasons.

Sometimes you might have the characters try the idiotic path and then come to their senses. Or rework the circumstances so that they have no choice but the rash move.

If your plot obstacle would disappear with a bit of common sense, or your characters look as though they are being stupid to keep the story going, you need to work harder to make us believe.

Why doesn't the character give up or walk away?

This is a similar problem. Sometimes when I'm reading a manuscript, I wonder: why do the characters keep going? Why do they keep putting themselves through such trouble?

Most stories need a reason why the character persists with their quest or ordeal. They must be compelled to continue – by influences in their lives, other characters or their own stubbornness, duty or fascination. Whichever it is, we must establish why they cannot walk away.

Perhaps they are trapped together in a neighbourhood, like the child characters in Toby Litt's *Deadkidsongs*, or the families in *A Thousand Acres*, or the world's last survivors in *On The Beach*. Maybe they choose to stay with troublesome people because they have a grand scheme, like Patricia Highsmith's Tom Ripley. Maybe they seek closure or can't say goodbye, or have become obsessed like the viewpoint character in *The Mask Of Demetrios*. Maybe they are in love, like Humbert Humbert or Graham Greene's Maurice Bendrix in *The End of the Affair*.

Many stories have a point where the character backs away, defined by Joseph Campbell as 'refusal of the call'. They're offered the adventurous path and decide it's too much trouble, or too painful. In Robert Harris's *The Ghost*, there are moments when the narrator decides the assignment is too dangerous and wants to quit. But circumstances force him to carry on.

Refusals are a useful way to bind the characters more tightly into the story. They also build anticipation for the difficulties ahead – and create the sense that there's no going back. Also, the reader roots for them to continue, eager to see what happens.

Give your characters a good reason to stay with the plot.

For your toolbox

✎ Any time a development looks convenient, try your darndest to make it a surprise.

- If your characters need something important, make them earn it.

- Look for moments where you might have despatched a story obstacle too quickly.

- If disaster strikes, prepare the reader obliquely.

- Beware of using the same plot-changing event twice without good reason.

- If a supporting character saves the day, make sure they have an important role in other ways.

- If you're using a coincidence to create a big finish, make sure we will believe it.

- Be careful how you use characters who blurt out important revelations. Don't rely on it as your only means of advancing the plot. Let characters make discoveries in other ways too.

- Look for the emotional dimension in a fight or action scene or make it a how-to.

- If you have a plot event or story device that seems to be obligatory, find an unexpected way to use it.

- If your plot obstacle would disappear with a bit of common sense, or your characters look as though they are being stupid to keep the story going, you need to work harder to make us believe it.

- Make sure the character can't give up and walk away from the story's trials.

8 Adding richness: do you need a subplot?

A subplot is a secondary story that usually features supporting characters, or a less intense problem than the major thread.

A subplot can add depth to a novel's world. Perhaps it examines your themes from other angles. By riffing on the issues in your main plot, you make the reader aware of them as a force of nature in your story, a resonant kind of weather that tunes the reader's attention to your subjects and concerns. *King Lear* is a clear example – it has a primary plot in which a king disinherits the wrong child and a subplot in which an earl has an illegitimate son he treats badly. The subplot widens the scope of the work – so that a story about a few dysfunctional families becomes an examination of misplaced trust and savage emotions, where the natural order is broken.

Conversely, your subplot might not echo your main plot at all. You might use it as contrast, perhaps to put the main characters' trials into perspective – for instance, as a foil for an intense and extraordinary story that might veer close to melodrama. You might use it to add the sense of real life, some short-term goals, mundane priorities and problems that will connect the reader with reality. After all, real life has this white noise. It doesn't proceed in straight lines with no distractions. We're usually trying to put out several fires at once. But beware of adding something that seems irrelevant; we'll discuss that in a while.

A subplot can give you a welcome change of gear to vary the pace and mood. If one storyline is unremittingly intense, a subplot could stir in diversions and complications that give the reader time to catch their breath. It can present natural spaces for characterisation, humorous moments or exposition. If your main plot characters wouldn't believably explain back story to each other, a subplot might give you other routes to reveal information.

A subplot is particularly handy for building suspense and tension. Once your readers are gripped by a story development, you can cut to another channel and prolong the delicious agony. A subplot is also useful for patching plot holes, giving you other approaches to solve problems or provoke developments.

And obviously a subplot can add length if your main story thread can't be extended without padding.

Having listed the virtues of a subplot, not all novels need one. Your focus might be so tight and your material so rich that the novel stands well without a second story. *Rebecca, Fahrenheit*

451 and *Flowers For Algernon* by Daniel Keyes are intense journeys through one chain of events and they don't lack depth, variety, verisimilitude, thematic resonance or a sense of solidity.

Or do these novels, in fact, have subplots? Certainly they have more than one thread. There are setbacks, trials and triumphs that are not the primary dramatic situation. *Flowers For Algernon* has a romance thread woven into the transformation of the main character Charlie Gordon. *Fahrenheit 451* has various friendships that act as barometers for Guy Montag's ordeal of change. *Rebecca* has the sinister, bullying Mrs Danvers. Is she a subplot, a plot layer, a device to enable us to understand more about various characters or is she part of the main mystery? In fact, she's all of them – which reminds us that stories are more organic than terminology sometimes allows.

The useful point is this. If your novel seems narrow or one-note, a subplot or another developing thread will add resonance, tension, complexity and scope.

Subplots that steal the show

Sometimes I read manuscripts that start out as one type of story and divert because a subsidiary plot takes over. Maybe it opens as a murder mystery and becomes a story of lost love. There is nothing wrong with that, if handled deliberately, but it must be done with care, not because you changed your mind. Also, be aware of what is expected of your genre. If you start by writing a thriller, the reader might be miffed if the secondary romantic story shunts the original quest aside.

With general or literary fiction, you have more wiggle room as reader expectations are more fluid. Also, the real interest is usually in characters and resonance. Having said that, if your themes change midway because a subplot becomes dominant, you'll have a harder job to make the book coherent – unless the shift is part of the main character's growth. (There's always an exception.)

If you do change your mind about the story, make a special revision pass to reshape the book. Sometimes we start with the wrong plot or protagonist and find a strand that is more compelling. If subplots push the main story aside, that can be a gift, a lucky development – one of the joys of discovery. Hunt down the threads that now don't need to be so prominent, or the plot questions that are now unimportant. (This is not the same as leaving plot threads deliberately unresolved – more about this in the section on endings.)

What if you have a subplot that is wrong for the genre, or overshadows your primary narrative? If you don't want to get rid of it, you could dilute its impact. Split it between two characters, or two sets of characters so that it shrinks back into proportion.

If your subplot takes you in a new direction, consider whether it fits your genre and edit thoroughly to fit with your new vision.

Subplot not developed

Even though the subplot is secondary in importance, it still needs to be developed. A subplot must have a sense of progression – a beginning, middle and end (more on this in the section on structure, p117).

Also, characters should be actively engaged in their subplot troubles. I sometimes see manuscripts where the subplot drifts along, as if the writer feels they must keep it at a distance. The characters don't commit to the subplot, never seem to take the initiative or move things on. Of course, this might be a deliberate choice that suits the needs of the book. Perhaps it reflects the characters' natures or the state of the world. But sometimes it's because the writer assumes the subplot should do no more than idle in the background.

Develop your subplot with as much activity and commitment as your main plot.

Irrelevant subplot

Spoiler alert: *King Lear,* William Shakespeare

Is it possible to have an irrelevant subplot? Readers are good at joining the dots. They will try pretty hard to find parallels and reflections to knit your storylines together. If you are writing literary fiction, you can suggest connections with very little. David Mitchell's *Cloud Atlas*, with its six nested narratives ranging from the 1850s to the far future, illustrates how you can encourage readers to find connections for themselves.

If you're writing genre fiction, you need to be more literal about the connections. Whereas a literary novel may not connect the various tracks of events except in the reader's mind, a genre novel usually has to bring the plots into direct contact on the page. They need to clash and affect each other – even if they strike out on separate paths at the beginning.

Remember the earlier discussion about reincorporation? If you reuse a plot element it creates a primeval sense of rightness. By the same principle, a subplot will seem more satisfying if it belongs emotionally with the story world – even at the literary and poetic end of the scale, as we see with *King Lear*.

To harmonise your main and subplot more thoroughly, try these ideas:

- *Mirroring* Use your subplot to echo the main plot or add contrast. List the similarities and differences and tune them more distinctively.

- *Make the subplot events enrich your characters* Humanise your people with a lighter side, create a love interest, or add a troubled dimension with a sinister shadow self.

- *Add a bridge character* If your two storylines happen in separate worlds, could you add a character who has a role in both?

- *Use the subplot to add complications to the main plot* Again, in *King Lear*, the characters of the main and subplots become entwined, with troublesome consequences. In the main plot, we begin with Lear, Cordelia, Goneril and Regan. In the subplot, Gloucester, Edmund and Edgar. Late in the story, Goneril and Regan become romantically attracted to Edmund, and Edgar joins Lear as an outcast on the heath.

There's more later on creating subplots in the section on games (p189).

Join your main and subplots together with common themes, characters and plot elements.

For your toolbox

🖉 Use subplots to add depth, thematic resonance, humorous relief, characterisation opportunities and complications to your main plots.

🖉 If your subplot takes you in a new direction, consider whether it fits your genre and edit thoroughly to fit with your new vision.

- Develop your subplot with as much activity and commitment as your main plot.
- Join your main and subplots together with common themes, characters and plot elements.

9 Story structure and plot points: let's twist

Spoiler alert: *Any Human Heart*, William Boyd

Structure – and pacing which we'll come to in another section – have a profound effect on a story's impact. Your events may be startling and your characters intriguing. But the way you play them is everything.

Stories aren't just any old sequence of events. They need to be constructed with peaks, crescendos and an overall shape. You need to generate a sense of increasing significance.

A good novel makes the reader feel they've been on a journey. That's not done only by dragging them through a lot of pages. It's not done with the number of characters you whirl in and out, or the number of locations you visit. It's done with an internal shift for the characters – by altering what the journey means.

This is what a plot twist is. It's a moment that makes the story events more important. It's an action or event that changes everything.

The point of ultimate significance is the climax – of course. But you also need a series of other peaks to keep the reader on their toes. There are classic places to deploy these that seem to work best and keep your narrative lively.

This principle works, regardless of your story's style or genre. If your interest is the characters' emotional voyage, your twists will be moments of major change in the way they feel and what they are compelled to do. If you're writing a thriller, the twists will be the scenes where the threat escalates most significantly. For a mystery, twists will be revelations or developments that turn everything around.

If you understand story structure, it will give you a critical path of when to play your major developments, what they should signify and how much emphasis you should give to the fall-out. A grasp of structure will help you shape your story in the most powerful order for your purposes.

Remember our mantra at the beginning: we are aiming for drama, depth and heart. Structure is the secret weapon.

So let's look at the simplest structure – beginning, middle and end. Hollywood talks about the three-act structure for movies – inciting incident, development and climax. If that raises your hackles and makes you mutter 'commercial' and 'formula', then pause a moment. Hollywood likes it because it works. It existed long before they adopted it as a master plan. It's the way people are wired, a fundamental grammar of narrative. Whether you're making a movie, writing an epic or telling a joke, you need a beginning, middle and end.

Why not two acts, beginning and end? Because you need the middle as a distinct phase to create a sense of substance. If the reader looks at the beginning they might think they can predict the end, but the loops and turns of the middle make them feel the material has been thoroughly explored.

A possibly confusing point: the acts aren't all the same length. The middle is twice as long, so it's more helpful to think in terms of quarters, not thirds.

Let's look at the kinds of event that belong in the different acts.

- Act one, the first quarter, sets up the world. It contains the event that begins all the trouble – known in screenplay circles as the inciting incident. By the end of Act one, the characters are committed to the story.

- Act two (twice as long, remember) is where the problem is being actively tackled and confronted. This is where the event that happened in Act one creates trouble and mess.

- Act three, the last quarter, is the climax and resolution, when all the trouble comes home to roost and the worst happens. In each of these phases, the stakes change, and the character's desires and outlook change.

Why are they spaced in this way? Readers (and moviegoers) seem to have an internal clock, and generally feel the significant shifts are most satisfying when played out at this pace. When I see a manuscript that has a slow beginning, it's often because the first major change – from Act one to Act two – is happening too late.

Another curious point about this frame – it's invisible unless you know to look for it. If you've done your job well, readers don't see it. They simply become more deeply hooked. Sometimes, even writers aren't aware of it. For every writer I've met who got the structure right by design, there will be another who did it on the feeling in their bones.

Structure may be well hidden. A novel like *Any Human Heart*, for example, is the story of a man's life, a faux-diary. It appears plausibly haphazard like a real life, but Boyd has used several structural tricks to hold the reader's attention.

The first turning point is more a sense of general adjustment than a pivotal event. Friends do things that startle or worry him. His mother loses an apartment because they cannot afford it. Lovers surprise him in unwelcome ways. But the middle has a clear and shocking twist – by now he has a wife and daughter, and he comes back from war to discover they have died. By the final quarter he has entered a desperate decline into loneliness and penury.

In case this seems too artificial, Boyd writes the book as a diary, which lapses for years at a time. This allows him to shape the narrative more artfully, as he can leave periods out and nudge the crescendos to the positions where they will have most impact.

He also adds more hidden support with the other characters who have arcs of their own – developing, prospering, ageing and dying. As well as enriching the novel's world, they also add a framework we understand. The brain likes patterns, and these other characters with their arcs give a sense of progress, landmarks in a wilderness. Some of the later events hark back to decisions the character made in the earliest days, which gives a pleasing feeling of roundness.

The book looks natural, but Boyd is using one of the most traditional and simple structures in storytelling.

So how can you use this knowledge of structure? You can keep it in mind when you outline the story, to make sure you're stirring up enough trouble. You can look for the pattern when you assess a draft for revision. You could edit on instinct, then check the structure if there's a section that's slow or too rushed. Often, if you reposition the major twists – or add one – the story magically feels right.

And structure is a guideline, not a hard rule. The proportions don't have to be absolutely equal. It probably won't matter if you begin your climax at eighty percent through instead of seventy-five percent. If you begin at ninety percent the ending might feel abrupt because you might not have time to slide down the other side. You might also have too much of a lull beforehand. If you crowd your pivotal twists too close together, the reader may feel you've skimped on the consequences. On the other hand, it might be perfect – especially at the end. Plenty of novels play a humdinger in the last page or so. Every book – and every writer – is different.

Now, to complicate matters, I'm going to tell you that the middle act – development – can be split. You might have a twist in the middle, and think of the story as four acts, not three. Some stories divide the middle even further.

Shakespeare split his plays into five acts – or four major twists. Use whatever model helps you make the best of your material. If you've identified five distinct phases to your story, or six or seven, it might help you to think of each of these as acts.

But if that's sending your head into a spin, just remember it all comes down to this: beginning, middle, end.

The midpoint – and stories with a sagging middle

In many manuscripts I see, the writer has planned a bold start and a cracking finish. But nothing for the middle.

That doesn't necessarily mean they didn't write enough text. Au contraire, they bravely deliver several hundred pages between the first incident and the last. Much of this seems to be aimless noodling until the sails fill and we're propelled into the climax.

In one chick-lit romance I edited, a girl got her dream job as PA to a glamorous film star. It was a promising beginning. The character then spent a lot of the book talking to her friends and hanging out with Desired Man. Nothing developed until, three-quarters through, she was fired and expelled from heaven. Then the story revived and we had a creditable rollercoaster to the end.

Between these two peaks, I could feel the writer was struggling. Her characters were kicking their heels until they could do their important scenes. I could feel her desperation as she tried to keep them occupied until the part she really wanted to write. She simply didn't know what should be in the middle of the story.

The midpoint – as we've seen with *Any Human Heart* – is one of the most important pivots. It shifts the whole dynamic of the story. Screenwriter Blake Snyder identifies it as the scene where the fun and games phase stops and the story gets serious. The German playwright Gustav Freytag identified the midpoint as a pinnacle where everything takes a hard turn for the worse.

In screenplays, the midpoint is usually an event – because that's what movies do best. Novels can be more gradual if that suits your genre, so your midpoint need not be a single dramatic scene. You can accomplish the same effect with a small tipping point. Perhaps the characters are aware of it; perhaps they are not. But at the midpoint, the mood of the story becomes more serious.

That's its essential quality. The events will have more significant repercussions – except for those that are being used as light relief. If you're writing a comedy, this is where the havoc is no longer lighthearted. If it's a thriller, the danger gets more personal or closer to home. If new elements are introduced, they won't be trivial. The time for triviality is over.

Suppose your characters go out for a coffee. In the early part of the book, this might be a simple, friendly scene. Past the midpoint, those same characters will be more burdened. Their approach to life will not be the same. Perhaps they'll find out who they can truly rely on, or in desperation, make an unwise alliance. By contrast, the earlier chapters will look like a time of innocence, or maybe naivety.

What kind of event might make an effective midpoint? It might be a false victory – perhaps the main character has apparently got their wish and discovered it was a shallow goal or there is a terrible price. Perhaps the original quest has gone horribly wrong and they now have to sort out a much trickier mess – which might be the true battle of the story. Your midpoint might be an echo of a scene from much earlier, but in a grimmer light – emphasising a transformation in the characters and what they want.

Another way to achieve this shift is to think about the characters' internal and external needs. If a character has been suppressing a desire, or refusing to accept an unpleasant reality, the midpoint is a good place for it to emerge. This is the moment where it can no longer be denied. In *The Godfather*, the midpoint is where Kay begins to discover irrefutable evidence that her boyfriend Michael Corleone might be capable of murder. From this moment she must acknowledge her fears.

So the midpoint might be subtle or showstopping, but it's the moment when everything turns grave. This is why it works wonders for keeping your readers curious. And its absence is why many stories slump in the middle.

To return to the writer with her story about the PA, she understood immediately what her midpoint needed. She wrote a scene where the narrator discovered her boss was going to marry someone else – which made her realise she had set her heart on him. This ticks several of the boxes we've mentioned. It confronted her with an inner need she hadn't been acknowledging. It was a severe challenge that would govern everything she then did. From there, the writer tracked backwards, creating scenes that would grow into that moment, and forwards to join it to her final crisis and resolution.

If you're struggling to fill the middle of your story, shape the events to create a shift in the character's priorities – or midpoint.

Middle is predictable or uninteresting

Sometimes identifying the midpoint doesn't give you enough material. You can break the story into logical steps that gradually reach the goal, but a story needs ups and downs, twists and turns. Remember we talked about stories that follow a predictable path? If a story is a straightforward journey from A to B and finally to Z, it will rarely keep our attention.

Look back over the discussion of acts and plot points. Notice not only that the story has turning points, but that the turning points add unforeseen layers of difficulty. A good story keeps moving the goalposts.

Take *The Devil Wears Prada* by Lauren Weisberger. The central character gets a job on a prestigious magazine. It turns out to be shallow and bitchy. Change one – she thought she wanted this job, but she hates it. She needs the money so she struggles on, but it's souring her relationships with friends and family. She hates it more. But then she glimpses a side of it that she likes, and starts to embrace the world. Change two – she's not just fitting in, she's forgetting her integrity. New priorities are taking charge inside her. Now she might have another aim – to become queen bee. And so on, down the slippery slope...

Moving the goalposts like this gives the story a pulse of its own. It keeps the reader rooted to your pages. I've already discussed how we need to get messy with our story ideas, explore the options, upset applecarts, stare boldly at the idea that's flickering at the corner of our vision. This especially applies to the main characters' goals and inner desires. Often, writers seem to envisage a target at the end of the book and write towards it, afraid to waver. But these changes are what turn the simplest situation into a story of depth and scope. Indeed, as I never tire of saying, they are the real story.

Create your plot twists by changing the characters' goals and desires.

For your toolbox

- Structure your novel to satisfy the reader's need for change.
- Check you have the three distinct turning points.
- If you're struggling to fill the time between beginning and climax, create a shift in the character's priorities – or midpoint.
- Create your plot twists by changing the characters' goals and desires.

10 Pace:
the storyteller's spell

A well-paced story is like an act of hypnosis. It has a travelling beat that takes charge of the reader's attention. It proceeds at just the right speed to trap them a little longer, beg them to turn another page. And this has nothing to do with the length of the book. Very long novels can gallop away with us because time flies when we're reading them.

This spell is cast by careful pacing – by creating a sense of tension and change. Just as the overall structure provides the story's major turning points, the pace keeps the reader hooked second by second.

You might assume pace is only a concern in fast-moving plots, such as thrillers. Not so. Every story will benefit if it is written with an awareness of pace; even a leisurely character journey.

Indeed, pace is a fundamental in most artforms – not just storytelling. If you're making a video, you want a change at least every fifteen seconds. The change might be subtle, such as fading a colour, or panning a picture so the view reveals more. Or it might be obvious, such as switching to a different image or bringing in a sound. Listen to a piece of music and you'll hear how it's being constantly modified. Even a simple verse/chorus/verse pop song, which appears predictable, is developing. Other instruments are joining, variations are being made with the phrasing, note patterns or rhythm.

Singers do it too. I used to take singing lessons, and I was taught that if a lyric is repeated, it must have different emphasis or emotion. It's the same when an actor repeats a line. The repetitions will not be identical (unless for a deliberate effect).

We can even observe the principle at work in visual art. Paintings will often hold our attention because they reveal more as we look at them. They are changing in our minds.

So audiences adore change. How can we do this in stories?

Always seek developments In every scene. The development doesn't have to be big. It can be tiny, such as the reader's perception of a situation or a shift in a character's attitude. But every scene should travel somewhere we didn't expect. Scenes with no change lie flat on the page.

Become aware of repetition Remember the singers and actors and how they are alert for repetition. Look for repeated lines, emotional changes and plot events. If you repeat something, develop it or make sure it will be interpreted differently – perhaps with new significance. (Unless you intend deliberately to keep it static.) Another type of repetition is the function of a scene, which is harder to spot. The surest way I've found is by making a beat sheet, where I summarise the entire book by listing each scene by its purpose. This reveals the kind of repetition that will stop the momentum. More about the beat sheet in *Nail Your Novel 1*.

Tune into your prose Pace can come from your style. Not from show-off words or sparkling metaphors, but at a basic, moment-by-moment level. Virginia Woolf said 'style is a very simple matter; it is all rhythm'. What might she mean? I like to think of it as the fall of syllables in a sentence. This is independent of length; a well-paced long sentence is as easy to read as a short one. But often we use more syllables than an idea needs; we cram in adjectives, adverbs and similes when we'd be better to choose a more vivid verb.

> She shouted in a harsh voice.

or

> She roared.

A smooth sentence makes every syllable count and uses them with grace. It has a quality of control, which keeps the reader in willing surrender to the writer's mind.

Pace keeps a story alive and restless. It sets up a discord, a need for resolution, a promise that there is always more to discover. When this stops, you let the audience go. And the proper place for that is … (meaningful pause...)

The end.

Let's look at ways to tune our awareness of pace.

Back story at the beginning? Think forwards

Earlier, we saw how back story can strangle a narrative if there is too much in the first act. But we need a certain amount of context, so how do we keep the reader tingling? The trick is to keep your eye on the pace. Devise scenes that will expose the background in the present timeline of the story. Then save the rest for later when the reader is more curious.

Shape your back story so that it keeps the forward momentum.

More pace, less speed? Rushing emotional moments

Spoiler alert: *The Sea, The Sea,* Iris Murdoch

Most readers notice pacing problems by saying a passage seems slow. But cutting may not be the answer. A slow passage may in fact be caused by the writer rushing the material.

Confused? Pace is nothing to do with length. It is all about engagement. When this falters, the reader's mind races faster than the material. They stop allowing you to take charge. So they tell you the story is moving too slowly.

Really, though, the writer may be going too fast.

This particularly happens with emotional moments. Although writers sometimes over-egg their intense scenes, they also err the other way and don't allow them enough time. This makes the scene look glib, or disappointing, or boring. Readers will go willingly and joyfully with a writer who has purpose. And if we rush, our dominance falters.

When an event or line of dialogue really affects a character, we need to give the reader space to be affected too. Time is elastic when it comes to our emotions. Think of the phrase 'time stands still'. The moments after an accident might seem to hang suspended for hours. In Iris Murdoch's *The Sea, The Sea*, a character tumbles into the waves. The period between slip and splashdown lasts for a page. Remember the car crash scene from Tim Winton's novel *Dirt Music*? It takes the character several pages to fully assimilate what has happened.

I've talked a lot about the reader's internal clock. This clock is not calibrated in conventional seconds and minutes, as a metronome might mark them. It runs on the inside experience; brain time.

In earlier sections, I talked about how characters react to shock and how wrong it looks if writers make them accept it too quickly. This is also how readers react to a shock, by needing to adjust and process.

So writers should pace an emotional revelation to keep step with this reaction. If a character tells her friend that her son died in a war and gives her his dog tags to prove it, the moment might take for ever. If a writer tried to hurry that reaction, they would lose the connection with the reader's experience. Like the character, the reader needs to take their time, confirm that it's inescapably true.

Readers may need to be nursed through vast emotional computations. They have to check they've understood what's happening, especially if they must grapple with disbelief. A well-paced story never races ahead of the reader.

Paradoxically, if you rush, you might be told the story is slow. 'Slow' is the default feedback phrase when we've lost our hold over the reader. But it doesn't always mean we have to cut material.

If a critique partner tells you an emotional scene is slow, check if you could enlarge a moment, dwell in it more.

Rushing: no context to help reader understand why events are significant

A variation of the rushing problem is when the writer hasn't made us understand why a development is important. But again, critique partners' feedback may mislead us into thinking we must trim when actually we should extend.

My agent told me that a sequence in one of my novels read slowly. I added several paragraphs. He said it read much faster.

It read faster... with more material.

What did I do? I added context. I made sure I'd expressed why the character took a particular action, the fears that motivated him. All this knowledge was in my head but I'd failed to put it in the reader's. And so for a brief period, the spell was broken.

We don't want the reader floundering to keep up or wondering why the character is fretting about something that seems trivial. And of course, we don't want to over-explain. Sometimes all you need to add is a beat of reaction.

> Did Stella always cough like that? Lou didn't think so.
> Still, he had more important things to worry about.

If readers tell you an important moment is slow, check if you have added enough context.

Too many emotional beats in a scene

Sometimes a scene has two emotional beats at the end, but there might be room for only one. This is something that's impossible to give an example of; much depends on what is happening around it. Sometimes, a scene will be dazzling if it twists and twists again. Other times, the extra beat will spoil the flow.

This happens in my work all the time, and I usually don't spot it until late in the edits, when I have the special ruthlessness to see the whole book clearly. Painful though it is, I rework – either into a separate scene or I cut it.

Are you trying to squeeze in a change too far? Perhaps you need to move it to a new scene or take it out.

Nothing is changing

I see many scenes of accurate, well-observed description that seem glacially slow. A character is roaming about a forest and describing everything they see, but the scene does not introduce anything new. Or a character spends pages weighing up every feeling and doubt. But he doesn't come to any fresh conclusion (and it doesn't serve the 'you are here' function).

These scenes read like first drafts, where the writer is searching to clarify their purpose. Most of us work like this – but afterwards we rewrite. We edit so that the scene propels the story onwards rather than retreading the same ground.

The exception is if the prose is so mesmerising that story was not the point. But even poems usually have a sense of development and conclusion. Pieces of music do too.

Readers are gripped by what is new, what is unfolding. They look for increments in every scene. They ask themselves why they are being shown a character going to the woods to have a think. Will he come to a conclusion? Will he discover that the problem has thicker tangles than he imagined? Or will the change be in our understanding of a character or a situation?

Each scene needs purpose – and it's best if most scenes are also purpose*ful*. For this, each scene needs a structure – and this structure is remarkably similar to the overarching structure a story needs. Something draws us in: perhaps it continues a thread we're intrigued by or presents something new and startling. There is a development (middle) that is not quite what we expected – on a grand scale or in a tiny way. There may be difficulties, reversals – all of which tell the reader 'stay with me, you don't know how this goes'. By the end of the scene there is a change. Again this may be significant or slight, but afterwards the character or the situation are not the same.

Whatever you show in a scene, even if it's a simple walk to the woods, see if you can give the reader a little more besides what they were expecting.

Scenes take too long to get to the meat

Writers often spend too long setting up a scene. For instance, a character takes her cat to the vet to get it vaccinated, and when she pays the credit card is declined. The credit card refusal is the important development – a shock that reveals the family is in financial trouble. Because of that she phones her husband, where she discovers another unpalatable problem.

But the writer describes too much of the episode. Opening the surgery door, putting the cat basket on the table, chatting with the vet, stroking the cat to calm it down, pushing the cat back into the basket, carrying it out again, talking to the receptionist at the desk.

Of course you don't want to rush the encounter, or give away the real point. But a well-paced scene will give just enough start-up to misdirect the reader's attention and then deliver the interesting stuff – the changes that matter.

I'm going to mention another useful scriptwriting maxim here – 'come in late and go out early'. Give us just enough detail so we think we know what's going on. Then get on with the change.

Vary the pace with a contrast scene

Although you want the story to be gripping, you have to be careful not to overwhelm. Readers get numbed if too many successive scenes have the same tone, (except in the story climax). A skilful storyteller senses when to ease the noose.

The classic times to pause the pace are after major revelations or ordeals, or if the characters are about to face an ultimate conflict. Release the pressure for a brief period. Let the characters gather their wits, or chill out around the metaphorical campfire. Perhaps it's a good time for back story. If the mood has been generally comic, strike a serious or sad note. Even Four Weddings had a Funeral. When timed well, these contrast scenes can enrich our attachment to the characters by showing a softer side, or deepening their relationships, and will intensify the impact of all your scenes. Another good source of a contrast scene might come from your subplot.

Use a contrast scene to let the reader recharge.

Kill your darlings: a precious scene that had to go

'Kill your darlings' must be one of the most famously repeated pieces of writing advice.

What are darlings? Anything that doesn't serve the story. By sod's law, it's usually the phrases, characters or passages we're most attached to. The classic offenders might be lavish, unnecessary description or overdoses of a lovable character, but darlings can also be more subtle.

For me, a darling is anything that hasn't earned its place and therefore breaks the writer's hold on the reader. Darlings might be anything we're reluctant to remove, big or small; their only offence being that they cause an unwelcome hiccup or repeated note.

For this reason, I find it helps to consider darlings as a glitch in the story's pace.

We often can't banish them until quite late in the editing process, when we're not thinking of ourselves, but of the book and its integrity. I'll talk more about that in a moment, but here's an example of a scene I was much attached to in one of my own novels, and why it had to go. I hope it will embolden you.

In the introduction to this section, I mentioned repetition and how it can weaken your hold on the reader. I cut a perfectly serviceable passage from *My Memories of a Future Life*. Its only sin was that it handled an idea I'd already tackled. The narrator collects a dress from the dry cleaner and remembers how carefree she felt when she bought it just weeks before. Now, though, her hopes were dwindling. Nice as it was, I realised I'd confronted that in a better way already.

So why the big deal? Because the scene had sentimental value for me. It was inspired by an heirloom silk velvet dress that belonged to my great-aunt. The dress was disintegrating because of its great age, and the great-aunt herself had passed that way long ago, so when I had the idea for the scene I was determined to use it. One day, though, I listened to my instincts: the scene was holding the story back. As soon as I slid it into the 'delete' file I felt the chapter ran more smoothly. In the end, I presented it as an outtake on my blog because the character probably still had that moment, around one of the corners of the story.

If I can get rid of my heirloom dress scene, you can be ruthless with your darlings too.

Before you get too drastic, consider that a scene can serve the story in a number of ways. A comic interlude might not seem to advance a quest, but it might be a vital contrast scene. It still belongs; very much so. An intermission with minor characters might reinforce the novel's themes and make it more complete.

Certainly a novel is not a machine or a production line. Not everything has to fit in a literal sense. And we risk sounding soulless when we talk about what is or isn't relevant. The apparently irrelevant interlude may have resonance, thematic purpose or just – simply – be entertaining. But writers need to be clear about why they're including the apparently unconnected event.

A story – short or long – that is edited with awareness of pace is elegant and persuasive. And that's a lot more compelling than a story with 'nice bits'. Look for passages that interrupt the flow.

What to cut? Tune into the rhythm of your story

Learning to cut irrelevant, slow or overlong passages is one of the most important ways to improve our novels. But identifying these is not easy.

One of my clients had a manuscript that was choked with explanations, back story, discursive scenes, flashbacks and general irrelevance. He scratched his head, saying: 'This is all important and interesting, I can't cut it any more'.

Stephen King tells how he learned to cut from his days as a sports reporter, when an editor put a red pen through his work.

I've also been a journalist, and it taught me how copy must serve a purpose. We would be given a specific linecount for a news story. It had to be fifty, not seventy-five. Not even fifty-one. Not even if all seventy-five lines were fascinating and useful. The story would be fifty lines because its subject did not warrant more; other stories had to be covered too. It had to obey the needs of the whole publication – like each scene in our well-paced novels. So I'd take the story of seventy-five lines and would wield the scalpel. And I learned this. There are always parts you can leave out. The story will still make sense and do the job you want.

News journalism is an extreme example, but all artforms work to limits – even novels. Novelists are working with the reader's attention – how long they will remain in thrall before they get fidgety for something different.

Every story has a natural pace. It can be fast, as in thrillers, or slow, as in more literary works (although not all literary works are 'slow'). Whatever speed your story goes at, this pace is what keeps the reader in a state of anticipation. It is a natural structure that dictates the highs and lows, the sequence of scenes and the mood – whether you should show a screaming chase or a lulling meditation. It governs the story in the same way that a time signature governs a song, or a heartbeat governs a person. If we break it, we lose command of the story – and the reader knows.

When we edit a novel, we have to tune into this rhythm. With repeated drafts, it tells us whether to cut from a scene or add to it; whether we have too much of one storyline and not enough of another; whether we need to ditch the digression and hasten to a development. It works at a micro level too, when we hear the beat of our sentences and paragraphs.

There is always material you wish you could have included

but did not serve the bigger structure. Look at the deleted scenes on any DVD. Some are trimmed because the film couldn't exceed ninety minutes. Others go because they tripped the story up, or kept the audience going round a loop too long. Jettisoning them was often painful. The director will tell you how they represented a lot of work – whole days on shooting, post production and music. How many of us are reluctant to remove a passage because it was a day's work, or a week's? Movie people know this pain and worse. They still delete if a scene doesn't fit the story's rhythm.

If this seems like an airy-fairy concept, let me assure you that finding this rhythm takes time. You might pick it up early in the writing, but more usually it becomes apparent as you polish. With some books I've found it on the second draft. Others, I've been adrift until I've rested the manuscript several times. But there comes a point where you understand how every event fits into a whole. The rhythm starts to sound, unmistakably. This is the beat the story obeys. This is what I must do to kidnap the reader from real life and keep them with me.

What if you've been through the story over and over and you haven't acquired this clarity? It means you need to edit again – perhaps with a break.

Discover what to cut by finding the rhythm of your story.

Pace yourself to edit well

Writing – and rewriting – like this is exhausting, so allow yourself time. Sometimes when I work on a writer's manuscript I detect a creeping sense of fatigue. Chapters start to rush. When I talk to the writer, they admit they were losing focus, even wishing the whole thing was over.

We can get away with rushing the drafting, but not the editing and revision. For that, we need to be fully engaged. We must also be patient with ourselves. If scenes prove difficult we might need to edit them in smaller chunks, especially if they are sketchy in the draft or need a lot of reworking.

Perhaps set a timer on your editing days – limit yourself to no more than a certain number of hours, and stop before you get exhausted. Only edit for as long as you can settle, taking every scene as it comes. And remember that as much sorting goes on in the back-rooms of your mind as when you're present at the desk.

Manage your stamina to edit effectively.

For your toolbox

- Shape your back story so that it keeps the forward momentum.
- If a critique partner tells you an emotional scene is slow, check if you could enlarge a moment, dwell in it more.
- Also, check if you have added enough context.
- Are you trying to squeeze too many emotional beats into a scene? Perhaps you need to move them to a new scene or take them out.
- Whatever you show in a scene, even if it's a character taking a simple stroll to the woods, see if you can give the reader a little more besides what they were expecting.
- Come into a scene late; exit early.
- Use a contrast scene to let the reader recharge.
- Kill your darlings: look for passages that interrupt the flow.
- Discover what to cut by finding the rhythm of your story.
- Manage your stamina to edit effectively.

11 Endings: surprising, inevitable, right

Spoiler alerts: *We Need To Talk About Kevin*, Lionel Shriver.
Lord of the Flies, William Golding. *Damage*, Josephine Hart.
The Body, William Sansom. *The Wings of the Dove*, Henry James.

What makes a good ending? If you're writing in a genre, you must deliver certain essentials. Thrillers need a high-octane battle. Detective stories must solve the case. Romances must get their lovers spliced (or forever parted). In a non-genre novel, you make your own essentials, but at the least there is usually an ultimate crisis that confronts the real heart of the problem.

A good ending will also contain an element of the unpredictable. We can't imagine how it will all resolve. If lovers are to get together, it will look as though the obstacles are too great. If a crime must be solved, it will look impossible.

How do you create surprise if the end seems obvious? In *On The Beach*, which is about the last survivors of a nuclear war, the end is obvious on one level – they will all die. The surprise is in how the characters face it and how we feel as we witness it – and how the book becomes an exploration of human courage.

A satisfying ending also seems inevitable and right. Any twists and revelations will seem fair rather than randomly invented.

A great ending will also do more than answer puzzles, knot the loose threads and confront the problems. It has a quality of thoroughness and closure – a feeling that nothing more can be said. Perhaps the monster is vanquished, if not in a literal sense, then metaphorically. Perhaps the heroes will be happier. Perhaps they have more self-knowledge, which may be a comfort but it might be a burden. Eva, the mother in Lionel Shriver's *We Need To Talk About Kevin*, is left picking over the debris of a long and terrible battle. Her husband and daughter are dead. Her social status is ruined because her neighbours – and indeed the country – blame her for the deeds of her son. In *Lord of the Flies*, Ralph, rescued from the island, weeps for the loss of innocence.

Your characters might not slay their monsters; they might discover they are monsters themselves. The jealous, obsessive central characters of Josephine Hart's *Damage* and William Sansom's *The Body* end their stories having discovered their own true depths. There will usually be a settling, a sense that the final ordeal has caused a new order. The last scene of *The Wings of the Dove* by Henry James has a line that is a fine maxim for any story ending:

We shall never be again as we were.

If you're planning an ending to a situation in which there is no obvious solution, this is a good compass. End when there has been a substantial change.

Should you tie up all the ends?

Spoiler alerts: *Blindness*, Jose Saramago;
The Kite Runner, Khaled Hosseini

Stories need closure. We've all been infuriated by novels that are deliberately teasing us towards their sequels – *The Hunger Games* and *Twilight* leave so many questions that the ending seems arbitrary.

In tying up the ends, we have to consider what the reader is most interested in.

In most genres this means revealing how the murderer got caught, how the romantic twosome got together or lost each other, how the world was saved (or doomed). But if we are writing a story that goes deeper than the events, perhaps we don't want to explain everything. Leaving the reader with questions might provoke them to join some ends for themselves, and the work may resonate longer in the mind.

Jose Saramago's *Blindness* ends when the plague lifts and people's sight returns, as mysteriously as it vanished. He pulls away at this moment, as everyone is confronted with what has become of their world. He doesn't address how society will be rebuilt and what will come afterwards. The moment of returning vision is powerful enough for his purposes, and encourages us to interpret the blindness in any metaphorical way we wish. No further events are needed.

In the Norwegian version of the film *Insomnia*, one of the characters tells an anecdote that is never finished. It appears inconsequential, perhaps a throwaway line to illuminate character. But good scripts never contain spare remarks, and this interrupted fragment resounds through the rest of the story, a signal to help the audience interpret what they are seeing. It is like the job the characters are doing – investigating a murder and having to create the ending for themselves. It is like the everlasting Arctic sunlight that won't allow the day to end. And so an anecdote left hanging is a rather metaphorical move. It's also a nice reminder that in some stories, the answers are not clear.

Let's go back to *The Kite Runner*, which piles on the coincidences. For me, they spoil the true power of its dénouement. Tying up too many ends actually puts the emphasis on the wrong thing.

Almost all the characters in the finale of *The Kite Runner* are revealed as actual figures from the protagonist Amir's past. The old foes are the persecutors of his childhood. Not only is this too unlikely for comfort, it seems to shrink the scale of this story back to a playground battle, and dilutes its power. Amir's central problem is not about getting even with a particular rapist. It is a more universal struggle, a need to settle an old score with himself.

There is a further twist. The wronged friend Hassan turns out to be Amir's illegitimate half-brother. This extra revelation seems unnecessary – they were so close in childhood that they were as good as brothers anyway. The duty of the close relationship was what mattered, not the secret genetics.

When we're plotting, it's natural to seek to join the threads and make every quest personal. We strive to show the particular and thus reflect the universal. But we have to be careful not to diminish, or solve problems that the reader wasn't wondering about. Some ends don't need to be tied. Fagin doesn't have to be revealed as Oliver Twist's real father. O'Brien doesn't have to be Big Brother, or Winston Smith's half-sibling.

Insomnia ties up most of its literal threads. It ends when the case is solved. But morally it is anything but neat. The characters exit with unfinished business and nagging burdens – and this is its true power. It is the toll paid by those who have to deal with murder. The viewer carries it too, as sharer of this experience in all its ambiguity. The story plays fair, it is satisfying – and it also deepens the mystery. The same goes for *Blindness*. Look again at Henry James and his closing line. Sometimes the person who will never again be the same is... the reader.

Would your story be more rewarding if some matters were left unresolved?

End is unsatisfying – have you missed the most compelling conflict?

Sometimes the ending fails to address the most compelling problem. This might not be spotted until beta readers or editors report that they were left unsatisfied. Or we might realise ourselves that our final chapters seem incomplete or lightweight.

Often, this is a signal that the story has further to go. Perhaps the final act isn't the true end, merely another stop on the way. Indeed, it might be only the middle. What would happen if you teased the events out further, challenged the characters harder? If you examine their needs, hopes and fears, what would be the very worst point? Have they, like Winston Smith, dared to follow their forbidden needs, been changed into a different person, then faced the direst consequences? Have you really got them there?

With *Lifeform Three*, the ending I originally drafted was reasonably entertaining, but seemed trivial. It didn't confront the character's most essential problem – a supposed utopia that made him unhappy. He failed the Henry James test. By examining the most fundamental questions in his life, I identified the way to his absolute hell. (And I ditched the final third of my first draft.)

Must the central conflict always be resolved? Indeed no. In some stories this is not possible. In Shakespearean tragedy, the conflict is enacted to its full extreme. Innocents perish, kingdoms fall. Finally, a new order blows in like a cleansing wind. On the other hand, we may accompany the troubled characters for only a short fragment of their lives. In *The Millstone* by Margaret Drabble, a young woman finds herself unintentionally pregnant, which throws her into a nightmare of conflicted feelings about motherhood and ambition. Does the lack of a final 'answer' mean that the conflict is not tackled? Au contraire, the problem is being confronted all the time. It generates everything. She is in a new situation in which she discovers who she is. (And she will never be again as she was.)

If readers and editors report that your story is unsatisfying, have you tackled the most compelling conflict as completely as possible?

Ending outstays its welcome

After the events of the climax, there's a period of winding down. If the characters go on to a new life, we might see them settling in. There might be secondary questions that wouldn't fit into the climax scene. A good place to resolve them is with a gradual reckoning after the main conflict is laid to rest.

However, it's tempting to linger too long. We often have a lot of material built in our imagination, further events and trivialities that we would love to share, and it's easy to write too much.

There comes a point where we have to hand the story to the reader and say 'I'm done, these people belong to you now'. Although the characters might carry on with their lives, we have to withdraw and close the curtain. I've seen many manuscripts where writers follow their characters too far into the ordinary. Once the urgency and intrigue has gone, the pace drags, dulling the book's magic. It's much better to exit before that happens.

As authors, we might long to write more scenes, because we can't turn the characters off. I've done it myself. After the final scene in *My Memories of a Future Life*, I wrote reams of material, convinced I had left something important unsaid or that I needed to give a character one more moment. Plenty of things happened after the book's final line; of course they did – the characters' paths were certain to cross again. But each time I added a scene, I felt the pace falter and drift. The important resolutions were done. I took them out again.

Our relationship with a book might be so intense that we write additional scenes as a form of exorcism, to clean the pipes. But they are often for us, not for the reader. Write them anyway, then do what I did – keep them in the outtakes file. You might find another use for them, perhaps in a standalone story or even in another book. Or they might stay hidden, known only to you.

My editor friend Victoria Mixon has wise words on this subject. She says a powerful ending flings the reader out of the story with their own epiphany – a moment that goes 'here it is, here you are, here's what it's all about'. The more complex the book, the more individual that moment will be for every reader – and that's who the ending belongs to, not the writer.

If you're tempted to write many scenes where the characters wind down into their new lives, consider whether they're essential or whether you should leave on an earlier, stronger note.

Ending with a different emphasis: the deleted epilogue from *Rebecca*

Spoiler alert

Daphne Du Maurier's *Rebecca* famously ends with the fire that destroys Manderley. But *The Rebecca Notebook* reveals that the novel originally continued into an epilogue.

It shows the de Winters living abroad in a resort, many years later. Mrs de Winter spends much of her time knitting, or reading to Max, or helping him to get dressed as he is now crippled. From time to time she strikes up a conversation with a less permanent guest, looking enviously at their baggage as they get ready to move on. The de Winters are stuck in a half-life, watching others come and go while they themselves are almost dormant. Funnily enough, it's a mirror of the life the narrator was leading at the start of the book when she was companion to a rich old lady.

Du Maurier decided not to include this in the novel. Why might that be?

In a lot of ways, it fits well. It has symmetry; the narrator ends up as she began, as invisible companion to somebody older and more famous (no one has heard of her, but Maxim is notorious). It's also consistent, character-wise, as this kind of life is what the girl finds comfortable. It's in her nature. We might also say she's tamed Max and turned him into a creature like her. There are many echoes and resonances in favour of this epilogue. And the logic works too. But still, du Maurier removed it. Why?

Because it changes the novel's emphasis. Without the epilogue, *Rebecca* is the liberation of this repressed, timid woman. With the epilogue, it is an anticlimax. All that emotion and angst has been for nothing. It's much more satisfying and powerful to drop the curtain when Mrs de Winter is finally free of Rebecca and the fears and threats she represents. It's a point of catharsis and real change. Even if the couple did eventually dwindle to this state, we do not have to see it.

In *The Rebecca Notebook*, du Maurier explained her reasons for writing the epilogue. She said her intention was to show a couple recovering after a great tragic event. Later, she said she decided that wasn't what mattered. It was, perhaps, an early draft intention... superseded once the book took another shape.

In fact, du Maurier did include elements of her epilogue in the opening of the finished version, but as small details. In this new position, they work in a different way, adding a sense of lost glory. So when you've been brave enough to delete a scene (or move it to your outtakes file), those moments are not necessarily lost. You may be able to slip them in, for another purpose.

Could you make your story's ending more powerful with a different emphasis?

End is too abrupt

Spoiler alert: *Lord of the Flies,* William Golding;
Persuasion, Jane Austen

For every writer who lingers too long, there's one who whips us away too soon. I've seen many novels where I felt the need for a gently paced chapter that allowed me to withdraw more gradually, mull over the remaining ideas and cross the remaining ts.

I remember one manuscript in which it was particularly clear. It was an adventure story, in which two lovers had been kept apart for decades. Finally, after the dust settled, they were reunited. The writer showed them alone at last – we had the briefest glimpse and the book ended.

I guessed – and the writer confirmed this – that he assumed we would know the outcome, would imagine the rest and feel the emotion as they came together. I applauded his wish to be discreet and to hand the moment to the reader, but it seemed incomplete. Why? Because we wanted to see this step in these characters' lives and we weren't entirely sure how it would go. The right words needed to be said. Bridges had to be built. The book didn't feel complete until we had reached the moment of harmony, although we might not need the whole reunion scene.

So when should you linger and when should you end more smartly?

Generalising is difficult because each novel is its own ecosystem – but here are ways to think about it.

If we are left with questions, what is their nature? Which steps are missing and do they matter? What must we be present for, and what are we content to imagine for ourselves? What is the story really about? Is it about solving puzzles and defeating foes, or is it about internal matters and the human condition? If the former, we will seek definite answers from the end, so the missing pieces may be frustrating.

Is it important that we feel the world is put right? One writer I know was asked by her editor to add an epilogue. Her characters had been through such terrible conflicts that she felt the reader needed a reassuring return to normality, a new hope. After the climax of *The World According to Garp,* John Irving writes ten sections of each individual character's fate, which fits with the scope of the story and the focus on their extraordinary lives. But in a complex work, the 'hows' and 'whats' may seem trivial next to the deeper observations that the novel urges us to consider.

How do we decide whether to, in the words of my editor friend Victoria, fling the reader out to take charge of the ending? We have to consider what the final notes are.

Is the reader's epiphany as important as the characters' resolution? Who does the end of your novel belong to? The reader or the characters? In a genre novel, the ending belongs more to the characters. Their puzzles are solved, their problems vanquished (or not). In a less straightforward story, the ending might belong just as much to the reader. Our own response and uncertainties might overwhelm the simpler practicalities. At the end of *Lord of the Flies*, should we see what happened to the boys when they rejoined civilisation? Or is it more powerful to end before that, on the moment of rescue, with the return of authority, civilisation and order – so we suddenly evaluate, in a nucleus moment, what we have witnessed?

With some books it's a tough call and we can argue in circles.

But let's return to the writer who wanted a restrained, discreet ending. It's still possible to do this while being complete. In *Persuasion*, Jane Austen shows the final reunion between the lovers as though she's filming it at a distance. We see that they got together, but the characters' words and facial expressions are not shown. It's satisfying and brings a final sense of rightness, but allows the characters dignity and privacy in their moment – which is all the more touching. The reader is distanced but not removed.

And the important thing – the reunion – is confirmed.

Have you ended your novel too abruptly? Would a final scene smooth the reader's path or get in the way?

Don't introduce anything new at the end

The ending has to come out of what has gone before. Once you're heading for the climax it's too late to introduce any new characters or subplots.

The most extreme example of this is the deus ex machina – the magic, unforeseen solution that saves the day. The villain is defeated because he has a fatal allergic reaction to peanuts or is hit by a bus. Or the protagonist escapes because she knows how to fly a helicopter – which has never been mentioned until this moment.

In Victorian novels, heroines might be rescued from their plight by an unexpected inheritance from an unknown rich aunt. But readers today generally won't buy such an invention so late in the story – unless there's a reason it fits. (David Lodge pulls this trick in *Nice Work*, and it suits his satirical tone and themes. Also, the main problems have already been solved. Not only that, the rescued character is a professor of English literature. The reader applauds the author's wit.)

In the early part of this book we looked at reincorporation, and how readers are profoundly satisfied when you bring back plot threads and characters you've already used. Readers are also deeply pleased by change, especially in characters and situations they're intimately familiar with. At the end of a story, there is rarely room for anything new.

The reader wants the finale to arise naturally and organically from what they have already seen. This helps create the feeling of closure and completeness.

Make your ending the result of what has come before, not a random external force or a late addition.

For your toolbox

🖋 Would your story be more rewarding if some matters were left unresolved?

🖋 If readers and editors report that your story is unsatisfying, have you tackled the most compelling conflict as completely as possible?

🖋 If you're tempted to write many scenes where the characters wind down into their new lives, consider whether they're essential or whether you should end the book earlier on a stronger note.

🖋 Could you make your story's ending more powerful with a different emphasis, like Daphne du Maurier with *Rebecca*?

🖋 Have you ended your novel too abruptly? Would a final scene smooth the reader's path or get in the way?

🖋 Make your ending the result of what has come before, not a random external force or a late addition.

12 Beginnings and prologues

Beginnings carry a lot of responsibility. At the beginning, the reader is a blank slate. They experience everything you show them keenly, like the first taste after waking. They take special note of every name. Here is where they look for the most significance, so you have to be careful to give the right signals. This is what goes wrong with beginnings – and how to get them right.

When you reach the end of your revision, edit the beginning again

I had a friend who was querying his first novel. An agent told him he had talent – but his first chapters had major problems. My friend replied: 'It's a pity those are the chapters I had to send. I revised them first. The ones I'm working on now are much better.'

You might be wondering why I've left the section on beginnings so late. It's because most writers fret about the opening too early. But consider what the beginning has to do. How can you finalise it until you know the whole work well?

Once you've revised a novel you've lived with it, played with the scenes, discovered levels and resonances, understood the characters and the problems of the world. You will also be editing a lot more strictly by the time you reach the end of the book, as you grow in confidence and clarity. To hone the beginning – and to know what it should contain – you need that disciplined mindset. You'll know what's important, what's irrelevant, what to emphasise and what can wait.

It's always difficult to introduce your book to someone who knows nothing about it – and to do it justice. You'll also find this when you write a pitch for an agent or editor, or a sales blurb, or when you face that tongue-tangling question 'what's your novel about?'. Sometimes we have to give it time, and wait for wisdom and familiarity to suggest the best answer.

Also, bear this in mind. The first scenes you write might not be chapter one, but somewhere in the middle. Although the reader is welcomed in through the front door, you might gain entry by a side window. Or the attic. If you think of an inspired start, fine – spring off the blocks and get writing. If you can't, find a point that gets your imagination cranked and begin writing there. You have miles to go and plenty to do. File a request for a great opening in the subconscious basement and let it report when it's ready.

When you've revised your manuscript thoroughly, you're ready to edit the beginning.

Prohibitions examined: starting with weather, waking up or looking in the mirror

These devices are often regarded as automatic sins. Equally, many writers use them stylishly. Their mastery tells us a lot about the essence of a good opening. Let's undo a few prohibitions.

Here's an opening with weather – *The Rapture* by Liz Jensen:

> That summer, the summer all the rules began to change, June seemed to last for a thousand years. The temperatures were merciless: thirty-eight, thirty-nine, then forty in the shade. It was heat to die in, to go nuts in, or to spawn. Old folk collapsed, dogs were cooked alive in cars, lovers couldn't keep their hands off each other. The sky pressed down like a furnace lid, shrinking the subsoil, cracking concrete, killing shrubs from the roots up...

Why is this a great opening?

It's assertive Weather is usually not interesting in itself. In real life, weather is often an empty conversational gambit – throat clearing, a request to start a conversation.

Hesitant writers often use weather this way, as they wonder how to introduce everything.

> Er, there was a blue sky...

But here, Liz Jensen has made extraordinary, eye-catching weather. It is weather that demands to be noticed.

Not only that, it's a dangerous setting, a war with the environment that makes living perilous. It skews the familiar – like that off-kilter opening from *Nineteen Eighty-Four*:

> It was a bright cold day in April, and the clocks were
> striking thirteen.

Liz Jensen's opening is about people We're more curious about people than we are about things. The opening of *The Rapture* is about characters and how their lives have been changed. Where normality is disrupted, a story is bound to happen. (In fact, this excerpt has a double dose of character because it turns out to be first person – though that's not apparent here.) It's also a good example of show not tell – we're feeling what the hot summer weather was like.

A storyteller is luring us in Openings aren't only about the events. Like the start of a song, they pick a signature moment to sell us the whole piece. Liz Jensen's beginning magnifies the interesting detail. It persuades us to lie back and be charmed. No one would wag a finger at Charles Dickens for starting *Bleak House* thus:

> London. Michaelmas term lately over, and the Lord
> Chancellor sitting in Lincoln's Inn Hall. Implacable
> November weather. As much mud in the streets as if
> the waters had but newly retired from the face of the
> earth, and it would not be wonderful to meet a Megalo-
> saurus, forty feet long or so, waddling like an elephan-
> tine lizard up Holborn Hill. Smoke lowering down
> from chimney-pots, making a soft black drizzle, with
> flakes of soot in it as big as full-grown snowflakes –
> gone into mourning, one might imagine, for the death
> of the sun.

How about starting your novel with a character waking up or looking in the mirror? Like weather, this can be bland, even though there is a certain logic in beginning at a routine point that will be easy to understand. The trouble is, this is usually set-up, not story.

If your protagonist is at the mirror because they've had a disfiguring accident and are getting used to their new face, that's drawing us into the story. This character's daily routine is a psychological place that's interesting to the reader. But if they're at the mirror to describe themselves before embarking an ordinary day, it will rarely hold our interest.

The Hunger Games begins with Katniss waking on the morning of the Reaping, a special time of dread and tension. It also fills us in on Katniss's role in the family and her hopes and fears. This is an opening that hits the ground running.

The Day of the Triffids starts at a moment of change – and a wry turn of phrase:

> When a day that you know to be Wednesday starts off by sounding like Sunday, there is something seriously wrong somewhere.
>
> I felt that from the moment I woke. And yet, when I started functioning a little more smartly, I became doubtful. After all, the odds were that it was I who was wrong, and not everyone else – though I did not see how that could be. I went on waiting, tinged with doubt. But presently I had my first bit of objective evidence – a distant clock struck what sounded to me just like eight. I listened hard and suspiciously. Soon another clock began, on a hard, decisive note. In a leisurely fashion it gave an indisputable eight. Then I knew things were awry.

A further problem with these opening gambits is that they're well worn. Readers are very used to them, and might not be grabbed unless you really dazzle. If you're pitching your book to literary agents or to editors at publishing houses, they'll be even more weary of them because they see them in so many manuscripts – especially the bad ones.

With that in mind, and to spur you to stretch your creativity to the very edge, I'll share this, which has to be the last word in wake-up beginnings. Martin Amis begins *Time's Arrow* like this:

> I moved forward, out of the blackest sleep, to find
> myself surrounded by doctors...

The character is dead and will move through his life backwards, so this scene is reversing out of his death. This does all the housekeeping you need from a good opening. It introduces the unique physics of the story. It spins with conundrums and poetic promise. And of course we are curious to see if he can keep it up.

Beginning a story with weather isn't the problem. Neither is looking in a mirror, waking up, getting dressed or describing a character. The problem is failing to be interesting.

Starting with a dream

Spoiler alert: *Rebecca*, Daphne du Maurier

Starting with a dream requires a cautionary note of its own. Why? Because at the opening of a novel, the reader is looking for the rules of the world – and deciding whether to commit.

The opening sets the ground rules. It tells us whose story we're reading and what kind of world it is. If there are purple talking birds, three-legged bosses or the character is flying, the reader might think it's a fantasy. If there are ghosts, they might deduce it is paranormal or a ghost story. The reader will seek clues from the tiniest detail because your novel is all new. If you start with a dream, you might create a misleading reality.

What's more, I've seen many writers begin with dreams to show off their virtuoso imaginations – hence the purple talking birds and other menagerie. Not all dream sequences are imaginative riots, of course. They might indicate longing or a vanished past. Dream sequences can be useful here, but equally, a dream might not seem as compelling as a 'real' experience. It's not the most gripping way to invite the reader in.

There are of course exceptions. *Rebecca* begins with a dream of the old house Manderley. It succeeds because it's a very realistic dream – like a vivid daydream. The emotions in it are relatable – a puzzled visit to the burned-out shell of an old home, which would be impossible in the book's reality. It's a startling moonlit exploration of memories and feelings, and very romantic. It also foreshadows an ultimate tragedy. And the character is clear that it's a dream – whereas another writer might lead us through the moonlit house and then pull reality away.

But as with the previous prohibitions, a dream may not be the most original way to open.

The opening tells the reader the rules of the story world, so be cautious about beginning with a dream.

Starts with confusing detail:
fights, battles and moments of high emotion

Sometimes writers begin with an overwhelming amount of vivid detail. This might be a close-up of the characters' inner lives, a tsunami of complex emotions. Or it might be a fight or a battle scene – we're dropped into the middle of a carnival of clashing swords, blasting guns or desperate scrambles.

Although this might appear to be a good way to get the reader's pulse racing, it is often too confusing. At the beginning of a novel we're trying to orientate ourselves. We're seeking certain basics. Who the characters are. Where they are. What year it is. Whether the story is set in our world, our country, our reality – and if not, where it actually is. These are the first steps to a connection with the characters. If we can't grasp them, a beginning of close detail or dizzy mayhem might be a meaningless muddle. We can't feel the tension of a fight if we don't know who it matters to or why.

But that doesn't mean you can't start with a dramatic moment if you shepherd those basics well. Here's the start of Andy Weir's sci-fi suspense novel, *The Martian*:

> I'm pretty much fucked.
>
> That's my considered opinion.
>
> Fucked.
>
> Six days into what should be the greatest month of my life, and it's turned into a nightmare.
>
> I don't even know who'll read this. I guess someone will find it eventually. Maybe a hundred years from now.
>
> For the record... I didn't die on Sol 6. Certainly the rest of the crew thought I did, and I can't blame them. Maybe there'll be a day of national mourning for me, and my Wikipedia page will say, 'Mark Watney is the only human being to have died on Mars.' And it'll be right, probably. 'Cause I'll surely die here. Just not

on Sol 6, when everybody thinks I did.

Let's see. Where do I begin?

This begins at a moment of intense danger – the narrator has just been left for dead on Mars. But before it plunges us into the struggle, it establishes the basics carefully. We have the time and place – a mission to Mars, a reference to Wikipedia that seems to be used the way we use it now. This is enough to tell us it's not decades into the future. We have the character's name, which also looks contemporary. The name also reinforces his relatability – he could be anyone we know. This short passage covers a lot of ground. Once it's done, we know where we are, who we're with and what sort of trouble he's in – and we're ready for more detail.

Some writers introduce their characters in moments of high emotion. Like physical action, this has to be carefully presented so that we can catch up with their anguish and share it, otherwise it could look melodramatic or sentimental. I see a lot of manuscripts, particularly young adult, where a first-person narrator begins with an intense emotional scene that is hard to connect with because we don't have the context. Indeed, it's usually off-putting, like witnessing a pair of strangers having a screaming row in the street. To them it's completely involving, but they're well beyond the stage where anyone new can be invited in to share.

So if we want to begin with an emotional situation, we have to pick our entry point carefully, and not too late into a character's emotional response. This is how W Somerset Maugham does it in *The Painted Veil*.

She gave a startled cry.

'What's the matter?' he asked.

Notwithstanding the darkness of the shuttered

> room he saw her face on a sudden distraught with
> terror.
>
>   'Someone just tried the door.'
>
>   'Well, perhaps it was the amah, or one of the boys.'
>
>   'They never come in at this time. They know I
> always sleep after tiffin.'
>
>   'Who else could it be?'
>
>   'Walter,' she whispered, her lips trembling.

This is Kitty and her lover, Townsend, in Kitty's bedroom, when there is an unexpected interruption. Kitty fears it's her husband. We don't have to know much about the characters to feel the tension. And more develops as the scene goes on. Townsend reveals a callous side, dismissing Kitty's worry. He doesn't care if he's caught or not. Kitty, though, is genuinely scared. What will she tell her husband? We also wonder what will become of her, because for Townsend it's just a game. We grasp the problems immediately, and the promise of drama to come.

When starting at a moment of intensity, don't forget to orientate the reader with fundamentals such as who the character is, what they are doing and where they are in history and place.

Starting with minor characters

Be careful if you start with people who are not your main characters or the main story. Readers pay the utmost attention to the people in the first scene. Also, they are auditioning them to see if they want to spend an entire book with them.

What about the novel whose point of view character is not the protagonist, like *Wuthering Heights*, which is narrated by the lawyer Lockwood? His opening chapters tantalise us with glimpses of extraordinary people. The focus is not on him, but on the mysterious setting and its intriguing – and frightening – players.

Much depends on the interests of your readers. Crime novels and thrillers often start with a murder or spectacular act happening to a character who may never be seen alive again. It is the event that acts as the hook and tips the world off its axis, rather than the people it is happening to.

If you start with minor characters, make sure they show off your main characters, or the main story.

Introducing too many characters at once

How many characters are you expecting the reader to grapple with at the start of your novel? Unfortunately, ever since Quentin Tarantino made *Reservoir Dogs*, I've seen too many manuscripts open with a large cast of characters who wisecrack and reveal glimpses of themselves through oblique dialogue. Usually it's a confusing mess.

I admit I came out of *Reservoir Dogs* wanting to whack more panache into my writing. But its opening techniques don't work in a novel.

Ensemble scenes are very tricky in prose. In a movie, we get extra information from the actors' performances and their visual appearance. In prose we have only the words. It's as if movies are super-fast broadband and prose is dial-up – the information is loaded into the reader's mind in an orderly line, not a wide, multicoloured spray. Some writers make it a policy never to have more than two or three people in any scene, regardless of where it comes – unless there's a pressing reason for a crowd to gather. If an ensemble scene is unavoidable, it's better to put it in late, when the reader knows the characters. Probably the most disastrous place for an ensemble scene is at the opening, where everyone is unfamiliar.

Of course, that doesn't mean you could never make it work. You might be evoking a scene through lots of people talking, making the ensemble act as one character – eg

> A murmur ran through the crowd. 'Did you see that?'
> 'Up in the sky?' 'Was it a bird?' 'A plane, surely..?'

It might not matter who said what and who they are. It matters that a group of people were thinking the same thing. But what doesn't work is when you introduce a lot of significant people at once, and try to make the reader follow what they're all talking about.

Of course, all is in the execution and how you keep the reader's interest. A great voice, for instance, might carry a scene like that (it might carry almost anything). But it is more likely that the reader will think: why am I being told about all these people? Are they important or are they just walking scenery? What am I meant to be picking up about them? Do I have to remember them all? Do I have to care about what they care about?

Be aware of how many characters a reader can pay attention to at once – especially in the opening scenes.

Hook the reader with head and heart

So how do we persuade the reader to stay with our book? The most irresistible beginnings snare the reader on two levels – intellectually and emotionally.

You can charm the reader with mystery, intrigue, drama,

comedy or atmosphere. Perhaps a body is found in a mysterious situation; a noise is heard every night at a particular time that can't be explained; a woman has an impossible love.

You could show off the high concept of your book, like the opening of *Time's Arrow*. You could set the scene with tension, like *Nineteen Eighty-Four* with its clocks striking thirteen.

You could begin with a character who will be significant and intriguing. Raymond Chandler's *The Long Goodbye*:

> The first time I laid eyes on Terry Lennox he was drunk
> in a Rolls-Royce Silver Wraith outside the terrace of
> The Dancers.

Or *Gone With The Wind*:

> Scarlett O'Hara was not beautiful, but men seldom
> realised it when caught by her charm as the Tarleton
> twins were.

Or begin with a place, like Ian Fleming in *Casino Royale*:

> The scent, smoke and sweat of a casino are nauseating
> at three in the morning. Then the soul-erosion pro-
> duced by high gambling – a compost of greed and fear
> and nervous tension – becomes unbearable and the
> senses awake and revolt from it.

Creating curiosity is comparatively easy. Snaring the reader's heart is much harder. We need a bolt of emotional recognition that binds the reader to the characters or puts us in their shoes. We need to feel what they feel. A lot of early drafts miss this.

Perhaps she is Everygirl, like Susie in *The Lovely Bones*:

> My name is Salmon, like the fish; first name, Susie. I
> was fourteen when I was murdered on December 6,
> 1973. In newspaper photos of missing girls from the
> seventies, most looked like me: white girls with mousy
> brown hair...

Alice Sebold goes on to sketch a picture of a recognisable schoolgirl – good at some subjects, disastrous at others, who is just discovering the wider world. These details are not just scene setting, they are hopes, trials and difficulties – the stuff of life that we all bond over. They link us to who she is – an ordinary girl who could have been any of us.

With a first-person narrator you have more leeway because they are our channel into the world. But if they are third person, it's a good idea to tell the reader something so they can start to form a relationship. Perhaps the character is on a tipping point to somewhere new and risky. Here's the opening of Marcus Sedgwick's *Revolver*:

> Even the dead tell stories.
> Sig looked across the cabin to where his father
> lay, waiting for him to speak, but his father said noth-
> ing, because he was dead.

With these few deft words, we're in Sig's shoes, sharing his frozen moment of disbelief, and his realisation that everything is changing for ever.

Or you could elaborate, ever so charmingly, on your title. Jodi Picoult begins *Nineteen Minutes* with this:

> In nineteen minutes, you can mow the front lawn;
> colour your hair; watch a third of a hockey game. In

nineteen minutes, you can bake scones or get a tooth filled by a dentist; you can fold laundry for a family of five.

Nineteen minutes is how long it took the Tennessee Titans to sell out of tickets to the playoffs. It's the amount of time it takes to listen to the Yes song Close to the Edge. It's the length of a sitcom, minus the commercials. It's the driving distance from the Vermont border to the town of Sterling, NH.

In nineteen minutes, you can order a pizza and get it delivered. You can read a story to a child or have your oil changed. You can walk two miles. You can sew a hem.

Having introduced the idea of a life of recognisable and average troubles, Picoult segues into the person waiting to snap,

In nineteen minutes, you can stop the world; or you can just jump off it.

In nineteen minutes, you can get revenge.

Thus warmed up, it's time to meet her main characters.

If you favour a more leisurely start, you could begin with a stylish flourish, like F Scott Fitzgerald's short story *The Cut Glass Bowl*:

There was a rough stone age and a smooth stone age and a bronze age, and many years afterward a cut-glass age. In the cut-glass age, when young ladies had persuaded young men with long, curly moustaches to marry them, they sat down several months afterward and wrote thank-you notes for all sorts of cut-glass

> presents... After the wedding the punch-bowls were
> arranged on the sideboard ... the glasses were set in the
> china closet ... – and then the struggle for existence
> began. ... the last dinner glass ended up, scarred and
> maimed, as a toothbrush holder...

We haven't see a whisker of the characters yet but we know their lives very well; the state of their battered marriage is presented as an inevitable progression, a law of the universe.

Both these openings establish a relationship through the voice of the book. Picoult's is smart and domestic. Fitzgerald's is wry and lyrical. We connect with humanity. That might be the characters, but it might also be the life in the author's voice.

For instance, the fragility in Sylvia Plath when she begins *The Bell Jar*:

> It was a queer, sultry summer, the summer they electro-
> cuted the Rosenbergs, and I didn't know what I was
> doing in New York. I'm stupid about executions. The
> idea of being electrocuted makes me sick, and that's all
> there was to read about in the papers – goggle-eyed
> headlines staring up at me on every street corner and at
> the fusty, peanut-smelling mouth of every subway. It
> had nothing to do with me, but I couldn't help wonder-
> ing what it would be like, being burned alive all along
> your nerves.

Here we have the time and the period; a wise perspective looking back; and a vulnerable soul beginning a significant journey.

To craft an irresistible opening, aim for puzzles and startling ideas, but also delve for humanity.

Prologues: yay and nay

Many writers want to include a prologue but should reconsider. Here are some thoughts.

A prologue can get in the way of the real beginning It's like starting the story twice. If your prologue features characters who won't be in the main story, the reader might feel cheated, or wonder if they need to remember them. Indeed, some readers see the heading 'prologue' and skip it, preferring to start with the 'proper' story. Some literary agents do too.

We've already seen how readers feel specially attached to the characters in the opening scene. It's like the first people we meet in an unfamiliar neighbourhood or a new job – they help us navigate an unknown place. The reader might resent you discarding your prologue people, and not have as much enthusiasm for accepting another cast so soon. Conversely, if prologue characters are less interesting than the main characters, you might never hook the reader.

Using a prologue to separate an event from the main story You might need to show your protagonists when much younger or older. Ask yourself: how vital is this event? And: is this the only way to use it? Could it be worked in later as flashbacks or a story within the story?

Or perhaps a framing narrative, like Michael Frayn's *Spies*, where an elderly narrator is looking back on youthful exploits.

If you can cut off the prologue and the opening still makes sense, perhaps you could shuffle the information in later.

Indeed, could you call your prologue 'chapter one'? Thrillers and crime novels might start with a villain who does not reappear until much later, or show a startling event that happens to a character we might never see again (quite often because they die).

Sometimes these scenes are called prologues and sometimes not. We could argue that the dream sequence at the start of *Rebecca* is a prologue, although Daphne du Maurier calls it chapter one.

Often we think we need to shepherd the reader with labels that tell us where a chapter is taking place, or what timeline it is. This is less useful than you might imagine. Sometimes the reader doesn't even notice that you've labelled a chapter 'Dresden, 1914' and that the next is 'New York, 1960'. They pay it no more heed than the numbers at the foot of the page. In any case, the real sense of time and place is created through the prose. It's your storytelling that conjures the experience of 1914 Dresden and 1960 New York. So 'prologue' might be a label you don't need.

Using a prologue to hook the reader with an exciting scene from later in the story Donna Tartt does this with *The Secret History*, opening with the murder of Bunny, which happens bang in the middle, chronologically.

It works well for Tartt, because she builds the rest of the novel around this. Part one, before the event, is narrated with hindsight. It ends at the point of the murder, and part two begins. The actual event is a gap, though it is much puzzled over by the narrator Richard.

But a prologue that showcases an upcoming development can be risky. Writers sometimes do it when they aren't confident about the beginning chapters, or suspect the book doesn't have a strong hook. A scene from later might be too baffling if we don't know the characters. It often has a tacked-on look and might even spoil the surprises to come.

Instead, should you rework the early chapters to be more compelling?

Using a prologue to give back story or information This is one of the classic uses of prologue. But beware – background and exposition, as we've seen, works better if it's threaded in when the reader is curious about it. On its own, back story may not be intriguing enough – and the expositional prologue may do you more harm than good. If you have extra background that won't fit in the story, it might be surplus to your needs. We all have back story that stays in our secret files.

That said, some genres are more forgiving of the background prologue. Fantasy and science fiction fans are eager to immerse in unfamiliar worlds, and might welcome a scene-setting preamble. A historical novel might benefit from a note about the factual basis, as might a contemporary or near-past novel based on people who really existed. This kind of prologue might be written in a more plain style, as an author's note, and distinct from the storytelling voice, so as not to start the story prematurely.

Such a prologue doesn't necessarily have to be dry. John Whitbourn began his alternate history *A Dangerous Energy* with the exam paper for the history BA at a fictitious university. The questions succinctly – and wittily – bring the reader up to speed on how history has diverged from our own timeline:

> 'Charles I's conversion to Catholicism in 1635 made a Civil War inevitable.' Discuss.

and

> Describe the three major historical schools of thought in the initial discovery of the magical arts. To which one (if any) do you subscribe and why?

Be aware that the reader might skip over your prologue and refer to it only if they get lost, or once they're firmly grabbed and want to explore around the edges. This is another reason to consider if your prologue should be chapter one. Certainly, the closer the genre is to the everyday world, the less patience a reader has for a background prologue. They would rather get it all from the story.

Using a prologue to introduce themes, concerns or concepts You might use a prologue as an overture, to distil the essence of your book in a way that helps tune the reader to your wavelength or themes. Earlier in this section I talked about the opening of Jodi Picoult's *Nineteen Minutes*, which emphasises how secret tensions might be brewing in the most apparently ordinary life. That could be regarded as a prologue because it is an introduction by the writer before we meet the characters.

I've seen writers go a bit mad with this, though, adding front sections on themes, mission statements and background. Often they're nervous that their intentions aren't coming through in the story. Sometimes the only answer is give the manuscript to a beta reader or an editor. Labelled introductions won't give your theme or thesis more impact; they might be ignored (see my previous remarks) or they might make the reader feel browbeaten. (They might make great blogposts or interview answers, though.)

So: to prologue or not to prologue? You might suspect that I lean towards the latter option. In our impatient society, readers are less tolerant of preambles and throat-clearing. They don't need a settling-in period before they pay attention. They are attentive from the first word. Also, they prefer to keep the flow. Moreover, the traditional functions of a prologue can often be fulfilled by more streamlined means.

As with any device, we should examine what we gain by using it or whether we are better being simpler, straightforward.

The fundamental questions are:

If you separate material out for a prologue, is your narrative improved? Can you make it enthralling and entertaining?

What was normal?

Don't forget to show us what normal life was like for the character. Stories involve disruption – situations that make life more challenging. So if you begin with a big shake-up, make sure we understand what is being disrupted.

I see a lot of manuscripts that begin with a promise of trouble, but give us no way to understand what impact it will have, or what it will change. This normality should be included in the early chapters. What might the characters lose – or gain from the event that starts the story? Why does it matter? Why is it threatening – or tempting?

So Somerset Maugham's character Kitty fears she might have been caught with her lover. After establishing them as characters (with intriguingly different agendas), we then see Kitty's everyday life as an ex-pat in Hong Kong, the things she likes and the things she is bored with, and how she is spoiling for a change. We also suspect that this will lead to a desperate mess.

A good way to show this normality is by following the characters' expectations. On an ordinary day, what did they expect to do when they woke up? The farmer expected to go out and milk the cows as usual. The hitman expected to meet his shady contact about his next kill. Kitty expected to spend another day trapped with people she finds dull, in a society where she is an appendage to her husband.

The characters' normality also makes the story relatable.

Kathryn Lyons in *The Pilot's Wife* has a family life with its average trials and troubles. She expected her husband would come home from his shift, she would bump along with their teenage daughter and life would bumble on in its usual way. Instead she is woken by investigators with news that he has crashed his plane. Soon he is under suspicion as a terrorist, and we watch her domestic security slipping away. Susie Salmon in *The Lovely Bones* expected to get through school, fall in love, grow up – and instead she is abducted and murdered. Indeed the book is heavily aware of the life she has lost – and the spoiled innocence of her friends and family.

If we don't see the characters' ordinary lives, we cannot feel the threats.

Establish what the character would normally have expected before the story changes everything.

For your toolbox

- When you've revised your manuscript thoroughly, you're ready to edit the beginning.
- Start with weather, the character waking up or gazing in the mirror if you can get us curious about characters, convey a state of unease and cast an irresistible spell on the reader.
- The opening tells the reader the rules of the story world, so be cautious about beginning with a dream.
- When starting at a moment of intensity, don't forget to orientate the reader with fundamentals such as who the character is, what they are doing and where they are in history and place.
- If you start with minor characters, make sure they show off

your main characters, or the main story.

- Be aware of how many characters a reader can pay attention to at once – especially in the opening scenes.
- To craft an irresistible opening, aim for puzzles and startling ideas, but also delve for humanity.
- If you separate material out for a prologue, is your narrative improved? Can you make it enthralling and entertaining?
- Establish what the character would normally have expected before the story changes everything.

13 Games to help you develop your plot

Thirty-nineish steps on the hero's journey: a question template to find your plot

Let's consider this – what makes a story?

At the simplest level, a great many stories start with a problem and end with its resolution. A lost item has to be found. A murderer has to be caught. A fear must be conquered. A memory has to be recovered or a secret decoded. A death has to be mourned and a new start made.

But it wouldn't be much of a story if the solution came easily.

So what else should it have?

Enter the hero's journey, as described by Joseph Campbell. Campbell identifies seventeen stages to the classic hero's journey, including the call to adventure, refusal, crossing the threshold, belly of the whale, refusal of the return.

Not every story will contain all of Campbell's steps, but almost all will contain this: an almighty struggle, in the form of physical and emotional ordeals.

This struggle is the story. The whole story. If you're having trouble creating a plot, look for the struggle.

Solving the problem must be difficult for the characters, and in a personal way. For it to be worth telling, it must push them to their very edge.

So here's a series of questions to help you transform your idea into a story. We begin with the obvious:

Why is your character's problem difficult to solve?

A struggle on its own is not enough. Walking for ten miles in the rain carrying a heavy backpack is undoubtedly a struggle, but it doesn't make us curious. Something in the protagonist's situation must hook the reader. Perhaps it is tragic - he's looking for a lost love. Maybe he needs to correct a mistake or injustice. Perhaps he regrets something or is being pursued by ruthless killers, like Richard Hannay in *The Thirty-Nine Steps*. Or maybe the problem is funny or bizarre, or gives us goosebumps (the character is seeing ghosts or glimpsing an alternate future).

What makes us curious about your character's problem?

Note these qualities – loss, regret, a sense of injustice, amusement, thrill, fear. They are emotive. We walk the story in the protagonist's shoes. Whether we like or dislike the central characters, approve of their behaviour or not, they are embroiled in something important and you must transmit this to us. We're not a fly on the wall, we're transformed into them.

What makes us share the character's emotional burden?

Let's examine how this works in *The Thirty-Nine Steps*, because it's a straightforward adventure that fits well with the hero's journey. The story opens when Richard Hannay is accosted by a stranger, Franklin P Scudder. Scudder is a spy who is looking for a place to hide after faking his own death. He tells Hannay of an anarchist plot to assassinate the Greek premier and destabilise Europe. Hannay lets Scudder stay with him, then finds he has been murdered and realises the killers will come after him too. If your story is more emotional, swap the physical challenges for threats to happiness and emotional safety. (Hannay's troubles are emotional too, of course. He might die.) Hannay has:

- *A reason why he must not fail* (he wants to stay alive)
- *A reason why he is likely to fail* (he's being hunted by spies)
- *A sense of urgency, a reason why this problem must be faced now*. This is essential because most people avoid confronting problems of great significance. Hannay can't let the problem drift while he carries on as normal. The killers won't wait. Also, he feels he must take on Scudder's quest and foil the assassination.

Why is this problem personally important to your characters? And: why must it be confronted now?

There should be a turning point that commits the protagonist to the risky path. Hannay could stay in London and hand the problem to the police, but he chooses not to because he is being framed for Scudder's murder. He decides instead to flee to Scotland, taking Scudder's notebook. There is no going back.

At what point does your protagonist commit to the quest?

Nothing should be easy for your protagonist. Hannay can't just go to the railway station and board a train as he is being watched by Scudder's killers. So he bribes the milkman to give him his clothes. Once in Scotland, he shelters in a remote cottage, thinking he's found a haven. But the next morning, the newspaper has a story about him and how the police have traced him to Scotland. He has to keep running. He doubles back down his original route, then jumps out of the train and finds his way to an inn, where he tells a modified version of his story and persuades the innkeeper to shelter him.

How does your protagonist's journey turn out to be more difficult than anticipated?

And: have you added the unexpected?

Hannay reads Scudder's pocketbook and deciphers his coded notes. This reveals that Scudder didn't tell him everything. There is a mysterious enemy group called the Black Stone and an important location called the thirty-nine steps.

In what way could you deepen the danger and increase the stakes?

And: could you add more mystery?

Two men arrive at the inn the next day. Hannay is lucky and the innkeeper sends them away. But his luck doesn't last, because they return. Hannay manages to escape, and steals their car.

If your protagonist gets an easy reprieve, could you transform it into a further complication, which the protagonist has to dig deep to solve?

When he leaves the inn, Hannay realises his pursuers have a plane, which makes it even harder for him to stay hidden.

On the run again, Hannay meets more people, who provide

more challenges and surprises. He has to escape from a village when the local policemen recognises him. He crashes his car, and gets unexpected help from the other driver, who turns out to be a local politician, Sir Harry, who bonds with Hannay because of his experience in South Africa and asks him to speak at a local election meeting. Afterwards, Hannay trusts him with the real story and Sir Harry writes a letter of introduction to the Foreign Office.

Don't forget how useful incidental characters can be. They might be kind and help your character. They might be suspicious of strangers and drive away, leaving your character stranded. They might have political or personal agendas and find your character is a useful friend – or a threat. They might be lonely and mad, and try to detain your protagonist simply because they don't get much human company.

How can other people provide plot turns, become unexpected allies or enemies?

And: if there is a bigger quest, such as Hannay's need to warn the authorities about the assassination, is there a way your protagonist could have a success or failure?

Hannay sets off again and has more near misses. The enemy's aeroplane is looking for him, adding to the pressure. He meets a rich motorist he knows from London and forces the man to help him. He has now become the sort of person who hijacks motorists.

How do the character's actions and thoughts show that the ordeals of the story have put mileage on him, forcing him into uncomfortable situations?

Once again Hannay escapes, and shelters in a cottage with an elderly man. But the man turns out to be one of the spies, and imprisons Hannay. (Joseph Campbell identified this as 'the belly of the whale'.)

Remember: people are unpredictable.

Hannay finds bomb materials in the room he's locked in (rather conveniently for my taste, but never mind). He escapes, but injures himself.

In what ways can your protagonist try to gain an advantage and make matters worse?

Note that these twists are not just unexpected events, they are triumphs and disappointments.

Are your plot events leading to emotional highs and lows?

(However, Hannay does manage to persuade a road-mender to shelter him, which is a tad convenient. But I digress.)

Once the protagonist has gone through several ordeals and had a major setback, you might make them wonder whether they can continue. How much do they wish they could turn the clock back or make the trouble go away? Even a brave, resourceful character might experience a dark night of weakness and uncertainty.

Can the character realise they may not have the guts or strength to continue? Could they have a darkest moment where they face the possibility of real failure? How severely can you test them?

Depending on the story and your interests, this is a point where they might be confronting their most fundamental nature and flaws, such as an emotional issue that has guided the way they live.

Now the character has developed, can you go back to the early chapters and knit some of these insights in?

And: do you see how we're enriching the initial situation?

And: if your novel has this scope, think of your character's real, core problem. Have you made it part of the ultimate challenge in the story's crisis?

If your hero has stopped to take stock, he can't mope. The crisis is coming. Despite accepting that he is broken, he must mend himself to face the final trial.

Hannay (who isn't particularly troubled, except for his injury) doesn't stop for long. He races back to London, meets Sir Harry's Foreign Office contact, Sir Walter Bullivant, and shows him Scudder's notes. The news comes in that the event they wanted to prevent – the assassination of the Greek premier – has happened. All is lost.

This is important. If the story had ended with the assassination being foiled, we would have felt disappointed. We knew all along that this might happen. So when it does, it creates a new crisis that whacks the story into a new gear – we genuinely do not know what the characters will do.

Has the worst happened?

And: what further problems will this cause?

Now the characters have to completely reassess their goal. Sir Walter holds a crisis meeting. As his inner circle leave, Hannay recognises one of its senior members as one of his pursuers in Scotland. From then it's a race against time to decode the most obscure parts of Scudder's notebook, find out where the rendezvous is, and stop the traitor handing Britain's military secrets to the Black Stone conspirators. All the threads are pulling together - the mysteries are solved, the enigmatic thirty-nine steps finally found, and of course Hannay personally saves the day.

This is a plot-based ending, as most adventure stories are. If your story is more emotional or multilayered, you have many ways you can play the end. Certainly we require our protagonist to confront the ultimate disaster and its consequences, and we must be surprised by the outcome. The end must also play fair and connect to events we have seen. If the rescue comes from a tangible object like a cipher code, it must also require emotional knowledge, gained during the struggle of the journey. A cipher code on its own won't do. We must keep emotion in charge – any twists must be triumphs and disappointments. Ideally, it should come from the problem the character was not equipped to face at the beginning.

I'll also add that an adventure story without some kind of internal change is dull – which is why the most popular version of *The Thirty-Nine Steps* is Hitchcock's film, which adds a romantic subplot.

Endings don't have to be happy or victorious. This depends on your genre, of course, and on whether the resolution is a result for the characters or an epiphany for the reader. (It might be both.) But to be satisfying, you must answer this.

Win or lose, has the story's struggle taken your character or your readers to the very limit? Once again, check back and reshape the early parts of the story if necessary so that they resonate in the ultimate crisis.

Those questions again:

- Why is your character's problem difficult to solve?
- What makes us curious about your character's problem?
- What makes us share the character's emotional burden?
- What would happen if he fails?
- Why is failure a real possibility?
- Why must the problem be confronted now?
- At what point does your protagonist commit to the quest?

- How does your protagonist's journey turn out to be more difficult than anticipated?
- Have you added the unexpected?
- In what way could you deepen the danger and increase the stakes?
- Could you add a bigger mystery?
- If your protagonist gets an easy reprieve, could you transform it into a further complication, which the protagonist has to dig deep to solve?
- How can other people provide plot turns, become unexpected allies or enemies?
- If there is a bigger quest, such as Hannay's need to warn the authorities about the assassination, is there a way your protagonist could have a success or failure?
- How do the character's actions and thoughts show that the ordeals of the story have put mileage on him, forcing him into uncomfortable situations?
- In what ways can your protagonist try to gain an advantage and make matters worse?
- Are your plot events leading to emotional highs and lows?
- Can the character realise they may not have the guts or strength to continue? Could they have a darkest moment where they face the possibility of real failure? How severely can you test them?
- Now the character has developed, can you go back to the early chapters and knit some of these insights in?
- Can you enrich your idea of the initial situation?
- Think of your character's real, core problem. Have you made it part of the ultimate challenge in the story's crisis?
- Has the worst happened?

- What further problems will this cause?
- Win or lose, has the story's struggle taken your character or your readers to the very limit? Once again, check back and reshape the early parts of the story if necessary so that they resonate in the ultimate crisis.

Focus on the struggle and you find the story.

Who has the biggest struggle?

The story exercise we just did shows how an idea can change in shape as you start to brainstorm. So is your main character still the principal interest or is someone else stealing the limelight? If so, should you swap them into the lead role? Or should you keep the dominating character at a distance and observe them through a relatable filter character like Watson with Holmes, and the staid narrators of *Wuthering Heights* who tell the story of Cathy and Heathcliff?

As your idea has developed, has a character grown into a more forceful presence? Should you switch them to the central role?

Check the point of view

In the original Nail Your Novel book (*Why Writers Abandon Books & How You Can Draft, Fix & Finish With Confidence*) I suggested at the revision stage that you check whether your story could be told from a different point of view or narrator, or whether it should be first person instead of third. This point has aroused contention, with occasional letters from writers who point out that the editing phase seems far too late to make that sort of change.

I guess, though, that they don't see how many books are

stymied because the perspective doesn't make the best of the story. With some novels, the point of view will be clear and obvious. With others, you won't find the most gripping approach until you experiment. I have found this to be a life-saver myself. With *Ever Rest*, my third novel, I initially intended to write a first-person narrative, and did much of my initial plotting with that in mind. After a lot of false starts, I realised I needed a sequence of third-person narrators to really work the idea.

As an editor, I have critiqued many manuscripts, way beyond first drafts, where the breakthrough came when we withdrew some of the intimacy and switched to a third-person account, or spiralled in to one flawed person's experience.

If something is wrong with your book, nothing has to be set in stone. Perhaps keep the events as they are and consider a new perspective.

Rock your structure

Beginning-middle-end structure is a perfectly good way to present story events. But what if you were more creative? Shifting the chronology might let you highlight other themes and elements of the characters' experience. Although plot runs in linear time, story doesn't have to. Here are some adventures to try.

1 Write each of your scenes on index cards and arrange them randomly

Does this give you unexpected resonance or contrast? Indeed, taking this to the limit, do you add an interesting effect if you offer the story as pieces for the reader to assemble in their mind?

Marcus Sedgwick presents *The Ghosts of Heaven* as four novellas, interlinked by an image – the form of the spiral. One quarter is set in prehistory, and is written in free verse. Another is a narrative of a witch-hunt in England. There's a section set in an insane asylum on Long Island in the 1920s, and the fourth quarter takes place in the far future, aboard the first spaceship travelling to colonise a new planet. The reader is encouraged to choose the order and make their own connections.

At the very limit of this you might get a narrative that is a series of fragments – like JG Ballard's *The Atrocity Exhibition*. In an introduction, Ballard tells readers they don't need to read the fragments in order and can miss out any that don't take their fancy. He is aiming for severe, jarring incoherence, but a fragmented narrative doesn't have to be so punitive. Your shuffling exercise might lead you to a new way to pattern your material, like *Cloud Atlas* with its nested, bisected stories.

If you use the shuffled events as an integral part of the story, you might end up with the time-hops of *The Time Traveller's Wife* by Audrey Niffenegger – although that novel has two structural threads because the main character's life unfolds chronologically and everyone else's timeline jumps around.

Or could you group the events by other common factors, for instance, according to decades, life stages or geography? What might happen if you gathered your material into sections that reflect a character's development, eg Hearing no evil, Seeing no evil? Fall, Rise and Fall?

2 Start at the end and work back to the beginning

As well as *Time's Arrow*, you can find this idea in Daniel Wallace's *Ray In Reverse*.

3 Alternate between points of view

Also consider the effects of adding a third-party narrator who can comment on the action.

4 Create a novel out of a series of stories

If you do this, readers will look for how the stories operate together.

Your stories might be linked by a historical (or faux-historical) endeavour, like *The Martian Chronicles* – which forms a picture of mankind attempting to colonise the red planet.

You might make the connection with motifs, such as Julian Barnes's *History of the World in Ten-and-a-half Chapters*, which has a recurring ship, and a woodworm who appears in each chapter.

You might connect the stories by a location. Geoff Ryman's *253* is about the two-hundred-and fifty-three people travelling in a London Underground train between two stations on a particular day. Each character has their own section, two-hundred-and fifty-three words long. It was first published online and in that version, hypertext linked you to other characters who are nearby or were connected with them. In the print edition, the characters are linked by an index. The reader can rove around these prompts or read from one train car to the next, but there is no fixed chronological order except in the final section. As a whole, *253* is drawn together by the idea of examining how different and how similar people are.

You might have hidden coherence, like Jennifer Egan's *A Visit From The Goon Squad*. Each chapter has a new prose style, new main character and new plot, and apparently abandons what has gone before. But after the end you realise that each of the plots was finished in the backgrounds of the other chapters and it clicks together after all.

Deviations from the linear are best done when there will be a bigger reward from presenting the story that way. So when you've made all this mayhem, ask yourself: is it an improvement or are you better with the straightforward presentation? Even if you ditch the idea of reordering your events, has this exercise revealed any previously invisible themes, associations or artistic directions?

Also, it's a good idea to make sure you know the linear version. Often I see experimental structures where the writer has got confused because they've made it up as they went along. This makes it incredibly hard for them to revise the novel, and test if they've put events in the optimum order.

Could a non-linear order improve the reader's experience? If not, might it help you see other patterns that you could emphasise?

Creating a subplot – from where?

Where will you find a subplot?

Complications from the fringes of the main characters' lives If the main focus of the story is the characters' job – perhaps they're detectives – generate a subplot from their family, personal problems, or a home with a big hole in the roof. Friendships and romantic interests can also put interesting demands on the main characters. If family is the core of the story, add subplots from your characters' work.

Inner life If the main story is about solving external problems – such as catching a kidnapper – subplots could grow out of a character's inner life. Perhaps they always wanted to sing an aria on stage or build a relationship with their estranged son. A subplot arc could arise from fulfilling this or accepting it won't happen. Or the character might have beliefs or issues that are tested by the main plotline, but aren't the central interest of the story. While this may not affect the main plot, you'll add a pleasing sense of roundness when the subplot is resolved.

Secondary characters Your secondary characters have lives too. You could create a thread for them that will collide with the main storyline from time to time, generating contrasts and complications.

Your central plot idea seen from another angle Shakespeare must be literature's favourite example of this, with *King Lear*. The main plot deals with the king who is disowning one daughter and giving his kingdom to the other two. The subplot has a father with two sons, one of which (Edmund) is disinherited because he is illegitimate. Edmund decides he's been badly treated for long enough. This creates a feeling of forces operating in the characters' lives, and thematic questions the story will be asking. The similarities also let you highlight differences in the characters' essential natures.

Create your subplots out of story dimensions that aren't the main plot concerns. Connect them to your main plot through characters, mirror scenarios and the setting.

Work your back story (and exposition)

What will you do with that great lump of back story or exposition? Here's a checklist.

- Make it into a mystery.
- Make it a character's secret – then have fun with the consequences of keeping it.
- Use for characterisation.
- Use it in a scene where the tension is mainly physical – if the character is defusing a bomb, let them tell the reader

about the explosives expert who taught them everything they know.

- Use it to bulk up the main story, like *The Secret History*.
- Save it for a bonding scene or campfire moment.
- Make character comedy out of it, as Robert Harris does in *The Fear Index*.
- Take it out, but keep it as a secret pattern that helps you understand the characters on a deep level.
- Wait until the reader needs a 'you are here' scene.
- Use it as background conversation to echo themes.
- Create a framing narrative and add the perspective of the character recalling a time of innocence (Michael Frayn, *Spies*).
- Split it into small, tantalising bites.

Several possibilities for the ending: how to pick the right one?

Since we might not tie up all the ends or spell out all the answers, where should we focus our ending? Brainstorm the following –

- the unexpected ending
- the predicted ending with an extra twist
- everything neatly knotted and fixed
- the ambiguous note
- the happy, the sad, the bittersweet.

How do you identify which to use? And if you have several plotlines, which should be resolved in the big finale and which can wait for a leave-taking aftermath?

Your main ending should involve the thread that's most fascinating to your readers. How much do they need clear answers? For genre fiction, this is usually straightforward. For non-genre novels, you might have many options, so your clue is in the beginning. What do your characters need, today, next week, in the long-term future? If they are headed for a tragic destiny, have they got all the way there? Look at your story's most fundamental question. What will make readers feel it has been thoroughly dealt with? If ambiguity or epiphany is your aim, which of your options will resonate most intriguingly? By playing like this, you might find your story is not what you thought.

Sometimes it helps to identify a final phrase, action or thought that feels right. Alan Garner describes how he doesn't begin writing until a final line emerges in his mind, at which point he understands what he is making. He may not know how to get there, but at gut level he has found the quality he's hoping for, a magnetic pole that helps align the rest of his material. In my own work, I find it helpful to aim for a final feeling and to ask: what has been revealed or defeated or added? Can the characters stop nagging themselves, for better or for worse? When I have brought the story there, I know the ending is right.

Find your right ending by considering your story's – and your reader's – most fundamental questions.

For your toolbox

- Focus on the struggle and you find the story.
- As your idea has developed, has a character grown into a more forceful presence? Should you switch them to the central role?
- If something is wrong, nothing has to be set in stone. Instead of changing the plot events, consider a new perspective.

🖉 Could a non-linear order improve the reader's experience? If not, might it help you see other patterns that you could emphasise?

🖉 If you decide on a non-chronological presentation, how clear are the connections? If they are not clear, is the lack of clarity intriguing and entertaining, and does it add to the reader's enjoyment? Or is it confusing?

🖉 Do you need to add anything to ground the reader? (See the section on *Any Human Heart*, and how the life arcs of other characters give a guiding structure.)

🖉 Experiment with repositioning an event or mystery, to re-lease its full potential.

🖉 If you're struggling to pick an ending from several possibilities, look for the characters' most fundamental needs and the reader's greatest curiosity.

🖉 Create your subplots out of story dimensions that aren't the main plot concerns. Connect them to your main plot through characters, mirror scenarios and the setting.

🖉 Does your back story or exposition have to be delivered in one large dose? Find ways to split it into palatable bites, or use it to bond the characters.

🖉 Find your right ending by considering your story's – and your reader's – most fundamental questions.

14 Games 2: where are you going? The synopsis

When I edit, I ask writers to provide a synopsis. This is for several reasons:

- if you're submitting to agents or publishers you need one
- if you're self-publishing you'll need to write a sales summary, and this is a good start
- it focuses your purpose to write it
- it tells me what the writer had in mind.

I promise I don't look at the synopsis before I read the manuscript and you should be horrified if I did. I navigate the book unguided, putting myself in the writer's hands. But in the synopsis, I often find a noticeable mismatch with the novel I've just read – so the book isn't working in the way the author intended. As good writing knows what it's doing to the reader, this is important.

Plot is not as described in the synopsis

I see a lot of synopses that do not echo the experience of the text I've read. There's often a major gulf between the experience in the writer's mind and what comes across to the reader. Many writers are feeling the drama keenly, but failing to convey it on the page. Here's a typical list of synopsis statements and how they compared with the manuscript:

Life becomes uncertain There is one conversation about money, then the characters resume life as normal.

Crime in the village is rocketing One character glimpses a headline about a vandalised bus shelter.

Lani is desperate She frets for a couple of lines before the muddle of her life proceeds as usual.

The community is up in arms Someone makes a disapproving remark about the characters' new garden fence at a dinner party. No other comments are made.

Theresa holds onto her job by the skin of her teeth Teresa tells her husband her assistant was made redundant, then office life becomes so unremarkable that she never has cause to mention it again.

George's accident proves to be a turning point There is one scene where the family seem a bit shocked, but then they carry on as before.

Jo is appalled by Bill Jo thinks about Bill on just one occasion.

Her mother's friends rally round Someone brings a pot of homemade jam one day, but apart from that there is no discernible change.

Richard and Thomas become embroiled in the Gunpowder plot Embroiled usually means to get into trouble. They didn't.

A lot of good writing comes from a process of questioning and analysis. What do you want the reader to feel? Examine it. Put the manuscript away. Come back and reread: ask yourself that question again and revise so that the story matches that ideal. When you can no longer tell, and you've had enough of cooling-off periods, give it to a beta reader. Check what they understood and what they didn't get. Show them the synopsis and ask if it matches what they read. Of course, their interpretations of plot events, character motivations and themes may be different from yours – but if they report that the story seemed vague or muddled by comparison, or the conflicts and dilemmas were not as strong, hone again.

Use your synopsis to check if readers are feeling the drama as keenly as you do.

Did you try to make your story sound more slick for the synopsis?

Of course, you don't intend to mislead, but how much did you pump up the story for the synopsis? Did you try to make it sound more gripping than it actually is? Often, we don't get clarity until we try to condense. The act of summarising makes us realise what we were trying to do and what should have happened. We might even get a breakthrough. If so, don't leave it in the synopsis document. Use it as cue to revise (again).

Obviously a synopsis will look more snappy than the full text of the novel. A manuscript has many more subtleties. It's the full holiday, not just the snapshot highlights. But every time we go over a story we know it better. That's what revision is – seeing it again. While we hone our characters, language and plot, we also clarify our own intentions and gain insight. And if at times your aim is to misdirect the reader, create mystery or obfuscate events, you must first know what you're obscuring.

If writing a synopsis makes the story snap into focus, try another revision with this new insight.

The fairytale synopsis: finding a plot in a muddled manuscript

Here's how writing a synopsis rescued *Lifeform Three*.

I was in big trouble. I was trying to revise my first draft and I had a file of outtakes that was significantly longer than the manuscript. My usual revision tools revealed a strong character arc, submerged in meandering explorations and too much back story. And everything was far too complicated.

More than anything else, I needed a stronger plotline to anchor everything. But I'd got myself confused with pretty digressions, mood scenes, explanations of the world and flashbacks.

Husband Dave had a brainwave. He suggested I write a fresh synopsis in the style of a fairytale.

> Once upon a time there was a character, and this happened, and he began to wonder, and so he did this…

And so on, seeking simplicity and clarity.

I wrote the synopsis from memory, without peeking at my notes or the old draft. This was a new outline from only the details I could remember. To make it flow, I had to find new connections. The results were very interesting.

I tackled the manuscript in thirds, looking for major turning points. Once I hit the first big twist I checked my beat sheet (revision plan) and added anything important that I'd forgotten. And voila – a purposeful route map for the first third of the book.

I tackled the midsection. Cohesion was the rule. Everything had to arise from the clear mission in section one and take it further. If I added new material, it had to germinate from the world, themes and concerns.

If a scene seemed trivial, predictable or uninteresting, it had one of three causes:

- I was pushing in an unnatural direction
- I was fudging with new elements when I should reincorporate
- I was forcing the development too fast – with more preparation, an event would develop organically from what had gone before.

Middle done, I tackled the final third. I'd written a big fireworks finale in my riffing draft and it didn't fit with this streamlined vision. I've mentioned this earlier, and how I junked the entire section and beheld the blank page. The solution wasn't instant, but I knew when an idea was surprising... but right.

You'll probably notice from this how ruthless revision is. We might jettison miles of material, even though it took effort to write. I removed scenes that were funny, entertaining or poignant; scenes that seemed strong when I originally wrote them. Undoubtedly they served as reconnaissance while I found where the true story was. That realisation is a writing lesson in itself, because some writers never realise how much they can improve their novel with a thorough, purposeful edit of the story shape.

Obviously you don't want to denude the prose. One of our maxims is that a novel is an experience, not a list of bare events. Diversions can be delights, layers and subtleties. But if you're in a muddle, the fairytale synopsis could lead you out of the woods.

How to write a synopsis with drama, depth and heart

Writing a synopsis is tricky. A novel might be a hundred thousand words long, and a synopsis must shrink it into a few hundred. A good synopsis should include the quality of the journey – the themes, the resonance of the setting, the reader's relationship with the characters, the lingering last impressions. Whether you're writing yours to introduce your book to the publishing world or to help your revision process, here's how to do it.

First, write the bones of what happens and where. Grit your teeth and describe these as straightforwardly as you can. Take a moment to lament that you have ripped out your story's heart.

Now we put the heart back.

First, get in the mood. Look at reviews of novels you've enjoyed. Find the thoughtful, intelligent responses written by people who explained why they clicked with the book. Notice how they convey this.

- They give broad strokes about the characters, saying one or two distinguishing things but not getting sidetracked by details.
- They are specific: instead of 'Emma is lonely' they would

say 'Emma is thirty-four and about to face another Valentine's day alone'.

- They home in on the novel's most powerful conflicts and the questions that keep the reader turning the page.

With this in mind, return to your stripped story – and add what makes it special. And as ever, if it's helped you see untapped potential or a stronger narrative line, dive into the manuscript again. Otherwise ... perhaps it's time to unleash it.

Study reviews of other novels to help you write a synopsis that does justice to yours.

For your toolbox

- Use your synopsis to check if readers are feeling the drama as keenly as you do.
- Did writing your synopsis clarify some of your ideas? Don't be afraid to revise again.
- Are the characters or plot more purposeful and dynamic in the synopsis than in the novel?
- If you're in a muddle, the fairytale synopsis could lead you out of the woods.
- Study reviews of other novels to help you write a synopsis that does your novel justice.

Appendix: top nine novice mistakes with plot

We writers are imaginative creatures of great ambition and originality. Especially in our first novels, we often bite off more than we can chew. We strive for depth and resonance, but it comes across as superficial. We grapple with the big questions and it looks insincere, or as if we lack confidence in our narrative. We stuff the text with ideas and it looks like a sprawling junkyard. We fudge technical details, hoping the reader won't spot that our plot idea is easily undermined. We use fancy devices like dreams, fantasies and books within books. We write snappy openings that captivate the reader but misrepresent the tone and style.

These discussions will help you understand the pitfalls of the novel medium– and how to achieve the effect you're striving for.

Story metaphor seems far fetched or trite

Not every concept works as a metaphor, or does it? Actually, most can. What we make of it is at least as important as the idea itself. Metaphors only work if they are used well.

There's a style of novel that uses community activities, such as musicals or quilt-making, as a way to bring characters together, to wrap the human condition in the processes of life. The characters produce a play or build a house. The ripening performance, the finished building, becomes a symbol of change. A metaphor for renewal.

Sometimes it doesn't work, though. The metaphor looks shallow. It never becomes anything more than building a house or putting on a show. What's missing? It's usually the dimension of significant change.

Here's an example, distilled from a scenario I've seen in a lot of manuscripts. We have a story about a family moving from London to rural France. They arrive, and the wife, looking for a new occupation, teaches herself to decorate furniture. There are many detailed chapters about sanding and scumble glaze. These are amusing for novelty value and because the character gets in a mess, but they swiftly become repetitive.

When I question the writer, I find she intended these scenes to have a profound significance. That's why she wrote so many – scene after scene of the furniture-painter's trials in detail. She intended resonance, but hasn't made us feel it.

She uses some other common devices seen in these kinds of

books, again intended to have symbolic heft. The character's children occasionally steal the paints. The author explains she wants to show a conflict between the artistic path and family responsibilities, but to the reader she never approaches this profounder question. The scenes never go deeper than the surface. They are only mundane and comical happenings.

The character makes friends with villagers. These should become mentors in the new world, or maybe antagonists that embody its dangers. However, none of them become important in the new quest – they remain as passing neighbours, wallpaper that makes the world look populated. The novel ends with the character setting up a business. This is certainly a result, but it's not resolution. Why?

We have seen no struggle on an important scale, merely the acquisition of new skills.

From the synopsis I know the author intended her novel to be a universal tale of rebirth, making a new life in a new place. But the story didn't involve life. The character's trials never forced her to make choices, or reprioritise, or form relationships that were outside her comfort zone. They didn't wake her up to a piece she was missing – or create a void that had to be filled or healed. The activity never became a millstone, or a task she had to complete at all costs.

Novice writers often don't realise what an author smuggles in to make the story metaphor work. And that's part of its charm, as we saw in the discussions of what a story is 'about'. Readers glide along the surface and sense they are also witnessing the profound. But this manuscript remained a story about painting chairs.

There was nothing wrong with the metaphor of the new start

abroad. Scores of writers make it work well, both in fiction and non-fiction. But this author's treatment of it was shallow.

If your characters' activities are to be a metaphor, include a sense of deep-level change.

Getting muddled?
When to stop adding ideas and themes

Novelists have to be good at invention. Some of us (myself included) are too good at it. If writing a novel is like cooking, you could go mad with all the exotic spices in your cupboards, but beyond a certain point you will muddy the character of the dish. The artistry is to squeeze maximum richness out of carefully chosen ingredients.

This is especially a problem for first novels. We get an idea, feel our way with it, usually learning to write at the same time. Every now and then we have a blinding revelation – a better plot twist, new and important resonances, an addition to the world of our story. Moreover, we get used to thinking the book is not ready. It doesn't help that most of us remember dissecting books to death at school in English class, scraping for every ounce of meaning and complexity. Usually we miss this: vast relevance is achieved with lean focus, not with sprawl.

There comes a time when your book needs no more new material. Honestly, it does not. Before you egg the plot again or excavate another level of profundity, ask yourself these questions:

- Have you got too many plot threads to tie up at the climax of the story?

- Are you using a lot of information-dump scenes to help the reader understand what's going on?

- Are some characters treading water because there isn't enough for them to do? Are you finding it tricky to choreograph scenes because so many people have to be present, saying and doing their bit?

- How many themes are you trying to highlight? There isn't a hard and fast rule about this, but themes work best by deliberate magnification. Magnification doesn't work if many other things are also big. Some writers cram too many themes in, and the book doesn't look deeper. It loses purpose and unity.

If the answer to these questions is yes, you may need to simplify. Look for the scenes, characters and story directions that make the strongest connections throughout the book. Take elements away and see if the story still stands without them. Indeed, it may be stronger.

If you've had a brainwave about a story idea or a theme, should you save it for the next book?

Inner conflict: keep it hidden

So conflict is the way to generate drama and trouble. But sometimes writers misunderstand how to use it. They write scenes where characters blurt out their worries in bitter arguments and yelling matches. This particularly happens in young adult stories with an unhappy protagonist.

They are possibly misled by TV soap operas, which often try to generate conflict with outrageous, uninhibited characters who argue all the time and never keep anything bottled up. This is not how most people behave (thank goodness). And soap operas have their own unique approach to story anyway. They are competing with distractions, the viewer's impulse to channel-surf or the need for feed-lines that are tweetable. You could say that soap operas are screaming against the rest of life to secure the viewer's attention. But novels already have the reader's full attention, so novelists can use their conflict in more honest and interesting ways.

Consider how to make your core conflict a silent threat for as long as possible. A state of disturbance that is difficult to ease. A secret that is eating the character from the inside. A love that cannot speak its name. An impossible choice the character is putting off. It will cause difficulties and shape the action.

Although the conflict might be confronted eventually, the torment must lie deep. It might be the root cause of arguments, but it won't be aired in the open.

If two characters share the burden of the conflict, this might cause an interesting collusion. Certain conversation topics might be off limits, so they'll express the strain by bickering about everything else. Or perhaps it will build a channel of tolerance and understanding.

An inner conflict might isolate a character, giving them special, peculiar difficulties. Perhaps only the reader knows how they feel – this understanding can be a powerful force in winning the reader's affection, even if the character is not particularly nice (Humbert Humbert, for instance).

The entire mechanism of a conflict like this is avoidance; internalisation. Not showdowns. Many writers rush to detonate the conflict quickly, unsure how else to use it. But they are squandering a compelling story point. Inner conflicts need to be paced carefully and kept simmering for a long time.

Minor conflicts, on the other hand, can be confronted – and in that case arguments might be ideal. But consider saving the major confrontation for the final act, where the character will be forced to resolve the mess once and for all. Note that word 'force'. It implies the confrontation is the last thing they want.

A true story conflict is not enacted through a meltdown or a dramatic row. Instead, think of keeping it on the inside for as long as possible.

Uninventing the cellphone: a convenient blindness about technology

Cellphones and the internet have made life easier and plotting harder. Motorised transport must have caused similar headaches. Gone were plots that hinged on the impossibility of travelling between towns, or getting about after sundown. Electric light must have spoiled a lot of storylines too.

We've got used to those, obviously, but we're in a cusp period with cellphones, Google et al. Some writers still try to ignore or dispense with them, especially if their novel has been a long project, begun in an era when we were less connected. And certainly these modern wonders can really muck a story up. It's hard for characters to get stuck or marooned, or stay out of contact.

But even if you don't use a mobile phone much (and in real life I don't), you must assume that most of your readers do. If your characters do not have this basic device and there isn't an excellent reason, readers will assume that it's because it would spoil your plot.

Some writers try to solve the problem with dead batteries or lack of a signal. That's been done too many times now, so only deploy if you can find a fresh twist. For every moment of effort you spend disabling these devices, you might be better finding other obstacles.

I read one manuscript set in a boarding school where the writer clearly hadn't wanted to update, and so she put a line in the early chapters to say the school was in a dead area. Not only did this look ridiculously contrived, it seemed odd that the kids didn't complain, or sneak away and find places where they could get a signal – because there would be a hotspot somewhere. This school also had no internet – which was a real sign of fudge. Unless there was a watertight reason for keeping the kids so isolated (there wasn't), it was hard to believe that parents would accept a school without this basic facility. If you're going to create such a place, why not use a historical setting?

Entire message boards exist to lampoon stories that wouldn't have happened if the characters had made a phone call. Many of these were in novels published in the past few years. You do not want to be in their hall of shame.

It's not just writers of contemporary fiction who do this. Authors tiptoeing into science fiction might invent a device that, say, teleports goods from the shops. However, they don't consider the other life-changing advances that might spring from that technology, or that high streets and transport would change entirely. Or they set a story in the future, then invent excuses for why the technology hasn't advanced beyond what we have now. Readers can smell the cover-up. It's like trying to uninvent the cellphone.

If we must get rid of the phone, we must do it cleverly. Perhaps the heroine is being pursued by a stalker and her phone rings. The stalker hears it and starts to close in. In desperation the heroine chucks the phone away, diverting her stalker and escaping. Then we will have been surprised and entertained, and will forgive you if she doesn't have a phone when she gets in bigger trouble later.

But technology gives us new possibilities, such as cyber-crime, identity theft and spying opportunities. We can write of struggles that are not ended if somebody has a mobile phone.

Dreams: part 2

We've talked earlier about beginning a novel with a dream. There are problems when we use them later in the text too.

First of all, why might we want to use a dream? For they are very tempting.

They're a chance to be more creative with setting, language, reality, whimsy, imagery. A very tempting opportunity to luxuriate in prose.

Dreams let you explore issues the character may not want to face in real life, either to give the reader clues or to prod the character to a new realisation (or strengthen their denial). You can dredge up forgotten memories or show flashbacks.

Dreams are also intimate and personal. Our real-life dreams are rich, random experiences that seem potent with meaning, very relevant to our lives but in a way that is mysterious. That would seem to make dreams perfect for a story – especially when we are so caught up in our characters that our time spent with them seems like an enchantment. Indeed our attachment to a dream sequence might stem from our own involvement in our story and characters.

So where do dream sequences go wrong?

On a practical level, the reader knows they are not 'real'. Dreams often don't change anything in the story (depending on your genre or subject, of course). The reader might feel it's wasted time. And if the dream does make a character do something, it might stretch credibility. Honestly, how often do people make an important action or decision because they had a dream?

If you want to show a memory or buried information, there's usually a better solution. Try a flashback. Or make a character find an old photograph, or learn something from a friend in a way that complicates their relationship. Or instead of presenting the revelation in one scene, you could sprinkle it through the story, tease the information into a mystery.

Also, dreams in novels can get too creative, as we saw in the discussion on openings. In real life, dreams are so delicious – a jumble of memories from the day's events, minutiae you never knew you'd noticed, wonky input from anything you've ever forgotten. The problem here is relatability. Although they might make vast, surprising sense to you, they are probably nonsense to anyone else. Certainly to create such an experience for the reader would be a creative tour de force, but the effect comes from context and recognition, not from the beauty of the images. The truest representations of dreams and their impact are usually found in magic realism – where they are, in fact, part of the 'real' action.

So if you use a dream sequence, be aware that the reader is thinking 'do I need to pay attention to this'?

Sometimes, though, a dream is perfect. Here's one my favourites, from Evelyn Waugh's *A Handful of Dust*. Scattered, absurd and vivid, it's a real cheese dream. A butler announces that the only way to get to the dining room is to ride the pony there. A discussion of buses turns into 'mechanical green line rats'. Characters fade into each other. It comes near the end of the book, so the figures are familiar and it serves as a poignant wrap-up, while also marking the disintegration of the character's life. Better still, because all good storytellers find clever ways to reuse their material, it has an unexpected consequence in the real world (which I'm not going to tell you…)

Think of dreams as a form of exposition. There are times when you've earned so much curiosity from the reader that they will indulge you. In that case, the reader might enjoy the message from the character's subconscious. But also ask yourself: 'is there another way?'

Fantasy sequences, parallel worlds, timeslips and genre mixing

The problem with parallel worlds and genre mixing is readers' tastes. Some genres play together nicely: romance and suspense; police procedural and thriller.

But some genres have conventions that aren't compatible. If you blend a contemporary narrative with slices of sci-fi or historical fiction, you're trying to please two sets of readers whose tastes might clash. Readers of historical fiction, science fiction and fantasy might want the world and its times sketched in minute detail. Readers of contemporary fiction might find that alienating and tedious. And the first bunch might find a contemporary novel too mundane; they want to visit an imaginative place that isn't the everyday. It's tricky to please both.

If the genres you're mixing aren't natural companions, you have to decide which you're strongest in, and make it your primary narrative.

Lady of Hay by Barbara Erskine has two strands: a journalist in contemporary times, and a historical narrative in the court of King John. Erskine begins with the journalist, who is hoping to debunk past-life regression. When she finds herself plunged into a drama that happened many centuries before, the historical narrative is softened for us by her sceptical, modern perspective.

When you introduce your secondary genre, whether you're time-slipping or not, stick with the traditions of the first. Don't try to switch completely to the second genre. This is where cross-genre goes wrong. Writers suddenly flip into high fantasy or sci-fi, deluging the reader with a narrative whose conventions they are not receptive to, and a style that's inconsistent with the story so far. (Jennifer Egan and David Mitchell are notable exceptions as they switch styles successfully, but mostly it doesn't work. And some readers don't enjoy this approach, even when done by Egan and Mitchell.) So if you're writing a romance that suddenly crosses the centuries, make sure your main character continues to search for true love. If you're writing a detective story, keep your focus on the mysteries and misdirections, and the suspects who might all have a motive.

So when you venture into a new world, how do you describe it? A good way is to make use of the connections with the existing story world, to make anchor points that are easy to understand. Iain Banks's *The Bridge* starts with a man trapped in his crashed car. Then we are into a fantasy realm which is his consciousness while he is in a coma. In the coma world are clues that tether us to the establishing scene. A snatch of delirious thought – 'the dark station' – becomes the first line of the coma narrative. The narrator has a strange, O-shaped bruise on his chest, which we, with our foot still in reality, know was from the impact with the steering wheel.

If you mix two genres that don't traditionally blend, choose one as your major genre. Use it to win your reader's trust, and mix in the other in an accessible way.

Stories within stories, books within books

As with dreams, the reader knows a story within a story is not 'true'. Of course, fiction isn't true either, but the reader agreed to engage when they settled down with the book. They didn't necessarily volunteer to read the characters' fiction (or spend periods in their dream worlds).

For a story-in-a-story to work, the reader needs to feel it matters.

Here's a fine example: *Tony and Susan* by Austin Wright. Susan, who is comfortably married with two children and a nice home, is sent a novel manuscript written by her ex-husband, Edward, who she hasn't seen in twenty years. Decades before, when they split up, he was a discontented drifter making incompetent attempts to be creative. Now he comes out of the blue and asks Susan to read his novel because she was 'always his best critic'. Susan feels awkward about it – and not just because she's worried the book will be drivel. There's difficult history between them. She feels guilty – and she's nervous of what she'll find in the novel.

So, when we get to this novel-in-a-novel, we're curious. What will we see Susan undone by?

This is the first rule of stories within stories: give us a mission, something we want to find.

Also, the stories should be together for a reason, adding up to more than their separate parts. Again, Tony and Susan has it nailed. The nested story is about an ordinary family who are driving overnight to their holiday destination. On a deserted stretch of road, they encounter a gang of kidnappers. Only Tony, the husband, escapes, and it is a story of literal, bloody revenge. The Susan narrative is about psychological revenge. Edward, her ex, knows she will be rattled by the ordeals he is writing for Tony. He is forcing her to have a relationship with him again.

Many stories within stories lack this crucial relevance, as if the writer hopes the reader will be patient enough to read anything put in front of them. Sometimes I wonder if the material has come from another cherished project, and that the writer is hoping the reader will indulge it if they claim the main character is interested in it.

If you have a book within a book, make the reader actively curious to see it.

Beginning belongs to a different kind of novel

Some writers start their manuscript in one style, then switch to one that is completely different. Usually it's because they are striving to hook the reader's attention, either with a spectacular event or an intriguing character. So they turn up the gas, then turn it down entirely after the first scene.

Certainly the beginning must grab attention, but it must be true to the rest of the book. If you begin like a thriller, that's what you prepare your readers for. If your story is more considered, interior and subtle, you should begin in that vein. Find something show-stopping, but in the same register as the rest of the novel.

Although you must hone your beginning to intrigue the reader, make it true to what will follow.

Tunnel vision: writer afraid to go with the flow

I strongly believe in outlining a novel before I start to write. It gives me a framework and a sense of purpose. I find nothing more demoralising than the suspicion that I'm turning out aimless scenes. (Some people don't mind that at all, of course. They are exploring. This section is probably not for them.)

But, although I outline, I need room to move. As I get familiar with the novel's world and characters, I loosen the plan, change the order of events, rework the characters' destinies. My outline then becomes a safe space to experiment, modify and adapt. When I revise, I adapt again, so that the storyline continues to twist, fold and evolve until the final draft.

Some writers stick to their outlines – or a core plan – come what may. This may work well, especially if you've done your homework beforehand. But equally it can also produce a sense of tunnel vision. Indeed, I see situations where writers actively try to block these moments when the story is begging for more development. Here are situations where we might need to loosen up.

I once assessed a novel that began with a community's annual feast. Tables were groaning with goodies. There was wassailing. But the writer had forgotten who his characters were.

The novel was about a community of Maya indians facing starvation because their crops were failing. The day's victuals were courtesy of a benefactor. So the feast should have had unusual gravitas.

I urged him to consider the situation he'd set up. How would those people feel if they were suddenly presented with plenty? It might not be glorious celebration. A character might look at the meat and drink and feel that to display it so profligately is obscene. Another character might collect up bread to take it home. Or how about some social conflict – what if the ordinary people got no feast at all, because they had to give the food to the priests?

I suspected this had occurred to the writer as he had a line or two that tried to dismiss it. He described the characters enjoying the munificence, mentioned that the food was donated, and that was that. But this didn't seem to fit with what people would naturally do. Their anxiety couldn't melt away in an instant. Their prudent, scrimping habits wouldn't be abandoned. They couldn't be. They were learned through fear.

When we discussed this, the writer mentioned that he'd had his eye on other things that mattered more. He didn't want to stop and examine that complication. And he wasn't keen to replace the opening scene with one that would be less provocative for his characters. But the issue needed to be tackled because readers would notice it. After all, we school them to spot situations that should cause trouble. And the writer knew this, really – hence his attempt to block it by telling the reader it didn't matter, that a good time was had by all. He could have rewritten the scene to make it better, without disrupting anything else, but he was so wedded to his original plan that he didn't want to. As you can see, it was unconvincing.

Another writer sent her protagonist to a writing retreat, where she discovered that a fellow student was her boyfriend's ex-girl-friend. As I read this, I was expecting glorious discomfort. I foresaw shifty moments in tutorials, uncomfortable feelings if they had to critique each other's work or see each other criticised. Instead, the writer patched the situation by including a scene where her two ladies agreed not to mention the boyfriend.

We discussed. The writer told me she wanted to show how well adjusted and mature these characters were. I felt that was disappointing. I also thought she was denying the more interesting and honest scenario. Wouldn't it be more of a journey – a story – if they achieved harmony after awkwardness and misunderstand-ings?

Again, the instinct to dodge the development is very revealing. The writer's conscience – or maybe a critique partner – often tells them there is a problem. They hope to dispatch it with a superficial sentence or two. Yes, there was a rape in the quiet neighbourhood of Sunnytown, but wasn't it lucky that no parents imposed extra curfews on their teenage girls? Then we can proceed with the plot as originally planned. Readers will sniff that out.

Sometimes you can't see that an event would spoil your plans or cause a bigger change than you bargained for. By the time you've written everything else, you certainly don't want to hear that. But there are only two proper ways to handle this situation. Either rewrite with something less disruptive – or embrace it and see where it goes.

Great plots aren't half hearted. They push an idea to the very limits of its skin. A fine example is Michael Morpurgo's *War-Horse*, which is like a grand tour of all the dreadful things that happened to the horses of WWI. Most of these ideas develop gradually, at every stage of the writing process, so we need to embrace them as we write. We also need to be alert for accidental signals we give the reader, and either adapt to them or remove them. If we block them with a hasty patch, the reader will stop trusting us.

Granted, a sudden inspiration might be severely disruptive, so how can you explore it safely? Sometimes it helps to examine how an idea might unfold if you didn't have to fit a pre-determined shape. Explore it in the manageable environment of a separate sheet of paper or textfile. List the pros and cons, without worrying about your master plan. You may reject them as wrong for your genre or story purposes, but you'll also find possibilities you've missed. Then you can adjust your outline and write on with confidence. Look for the dramatic possibilities beyond your original story outline. If an incident should change something, don't smother it – see where it takes you.

For your toolbox

- If your characters' activities are to be a metaphor, you must include a sense of deep-level change.
- If you've had a brainwave about a story idea or a theme, should you save it for the next book?
- A true story conflict is not enacted through a meltdown or a dramatic row. Keep it bottled up for as long as possible.
- While we can sometimes maroon our characters away from the internet or cellphones, we should also write of new struggles, such as cyber-crime and spying opportunities.
- Think of dream sequences as a form of exposition. There are times when you've earned so much curiosity that the reader will enjoy a message from the character's subconscious. But also ask yourself: 'is there another way to show this?'
- If you mix two genres that don't traditionally blend, choose one as your major genre. Use it to win your reader's trust, and mix in the other in an accessible way.
- If you have a book within a book, make the reader actively curious to see it.
- Although you must hone your beginning to intrigue the reader, make sure it's also true to what is to come.
- Look for the dramatic possibilities beyond your original story outline. If an incident should change something, don't smother it – experiment in a separate document.

Index

About the author

Roz Morris has more than a dozen published novels under her belt. She has a secret identity as a ghostwriter and her titles have sold more than four million copies worldwide. She is also coming out of the shadows with critically acclaimed novels of her own: *My Memories of a Future Life* and *Lifeform Three*.

Roz is also a tutor on the *Guardian* newspaper creative writing courses and she mentors other writers. One manuscript she doctored in early form won the Roald Dahl Funny Prize 2012. She began her Nail Your Novel series in response to the most frequent problems her clients encounter.

Another Nail Your Novel book is in the works, and Roz always has novels of her own to nail. Connect with her on Twitter at @Roz_Morris, on her website rozmorris.wordpress.com and on her blog www.nailyournovel.com

If you've enjoyed this book, would you consider leaving a review on line? It makes all the difference to independent publishers who rely on word of mouth to get their books known. Thank you!

Nail Your Novel: Why Writers Abandon Books and How You Can Draft, Fix and Finish With Confidence

'Should be used as a text in writing courses'

'There are shedloads of books on how to write novels, and a lot are longer and considerably less useful'

Are you writing a novel? Do you want to make sure you finish? Will you get lost and fizzle out? Will you spend more time reading about how to write than getting words down?

Most books on novel-writing make you read hundreds of pages about arcs, inciting incidents, heroes' journeys. It's great to know that – but that's not writing your book. In ten steps Nail Your Novel will tell you how to:

- shape your big idea and make a novel out of it
- use research
- organise your time
- write when you don't feel inspired
- reread what you've written and polish it.

You don't even need to read the whole book before you get started. You read a section, then do as it says. And, once you're finally satisfied, Nail Your Novel will tell you how to present it to publishers and agents, should you wish to. You've dreamed of writing a novel. Don't procrastinate with another theory book. Don't launch in, get stuck and throw your hard work in a drawer. Draft, fix and finish with confidence.

Available in e-editions and in print.

Writing Characters Who'll Keep Readers Captivated: Nail Your Novel 2

How do you create characters who keep readers hooked? How do you write the opposite sex? Teenagers? Believable relationships? Historical characters? Enigmatic characters? Plausible antagonists and chilling villains?

How do you understand a character whose life is totally unlike your own? People who live in dystopias? What makes dialogue sing? When can you let the reader intuit what the characters are feeling and when should you spell it out?

Whether you write a story-based genre or literary fiction, people are the heart of any novel. Using tutorials, games and exercises, this book will show you how to create characters who will bewitch readers – and make you want to tell stories.

'From designing central characters to managing the 'extras' in your cast, every aspect of character creation is illumined. And Morris's colloquial style frees the writer from being tangled up in technicalities.'

My Memories of a Future Life

'Taut plotting and sharp storytelling'
'Classy, stylish writing... a profound tale in page-turning fashion'
'Amusing, mysterious, surreal and intense'

If your life was somebody's past, what echoes would you leave in their soul? Could they be the answers you need now?

It's a question Carol never expected to face. She's a gifted musician who needs nothing more than her piano. She certainly doesn't think she's ever lived before. But forced by injury to stop playing, she fears her life may be over. Enter her soulmate Andreq; healer, liar, fraud and loyal friend. Is he her future incarnation or a psychological figment? And can his story help her discover how to live now?

'Much more than a twist on the traditional reincarnation tale...'
'A stunning achievement... like Doris Lessing but much more readable'

Available in ebook, audiobook and print.
MyMemoriesOfAFutureLife.com

Lifeform Three

'Beautifully written; meaningful. Top-drawer storytelling in the tradition of Atwood and Bradbury'
'Spellbinding... charming, engrossing, uplifting'
'I really didn't want this book to end. It's that good'

Misty woods; abandoned towns; secrets in the landscape; a forbidden life by night; the scent of bygone days; a past that lies below the surface; and a door in a dream that seems to hold the answers.

Paftoo is a 'bod'; made to serve. He is a groundsman on the last remaining countryside estate, once known as Harkaway Hall – now a theme park. Paftoo holds scattered memories of the old days, but they are regularly deleted to keep him productive.

When he starts to have dreams of the Lost Lands' past and his cherished connection with Lifeform Three, Paftoo is propelled into a nightly battle to reclaim his memories, his former companions and his soul.

'Reminded me of Never Let Me Go by Kazuo Ishiguro, but Lifeform Three is much more joyous and less tragic.'

Includes an appendix of suggested questions for reading groups.
Available in ebook, audiobook and in print.
Lifeformthree.com

Made in the USA
Columbia, SC
20 March 2019